by **D.D. Dunn**

Cobwebs
Critters
'n Coveralls

Homegrown Humor
from the **Heartland**

Mark My Words
PRESS

Cover photo and other farm images in the book are
pictures of Dunn Movin' Farm,
taken the day we moved in, June 12, 1963.

Cover, book design and typography:
Janet Pulvermacher

Published by
Mark My Words Press
PO Box 44847, Madison, WI 53744-4847
800-342-4404

Printed in the United States of America

To my folks, Gene and Jean,
who taught me to laugh
at every opportunity;
and to Nancy,
who was once just my sister,
and is now my cherished friend.

Thanks
for filling my life with so much
love and laughter...

Acknowledgments

I want to thank God for all of the blessings He has poured out on my life.

And to Marc and Elizabeth who constantly remind me of the joy of each day.

To Janet, who keeps working with me even when I am impossible to work with…and does an outstanding job in spite of me (Hey DD…it's *because* of you that I even come close to doing an outstanding job!).

To Jane, Kathy and the staff at the Illinois Prairie Area Library System—without you I would have never gotten this far…and had this much fun.

To all the librarians, teachers, students and other community members who have taken time from their busy schedules to visit with me on the "Binder Twine 'n Bandaids" tour, your hospitality was overwhelming!

And to you…all of you readers…who have curled up on the couch or in some other comfy spot to read one or two of my stories.

Thank you all,
from the bottom of my heart!

A note from the author...

Hmmmm... it's probably time to get on with that next book. "Movin' out, movin' up and movin' on."

I've got plenty of more stories I still need to share. 'Bout how I got my rear-end stuck between the dash and the windshield of the car, 'bout the stretchy doll that could only go so far, and 'bout all the other things our kids have done. I want to remember to tell you 'bout the goats that got my husband down on the ground at the petting zoo, and how I got stuck in the roller coaster car. Yep, there's plenty more stuff for us to talk about.

I'll get to it some sunny summer day when the sunbeams are falling through the clouds, and I am sitting in the grass drinking a sweet tea.

Then...
we can get together and talk
about my stories...
and yours.

D.D. Dunn
Davenport, IA

Table of Contents

CHAPTER
ONE

COBWEBS
'n'
CRITTERS

S o, there we were. Standing in front of a house that looked like it should have been condemned. As my eyes scanned over the property from the house to the barns to the sheds…well…it was just more than my seven year old brain could take in. Why were we moving from a real house—with running water and heat—to a place like this? What the heck were my folks thinking?

But the deal was already sealed. The previous owners were loading up two horses that had been staying in the house we were actually going to move into. All I could think was 'what a rip-off' because obviously the horses were the best part of the bargain and they were taking them!

I looked over at my brother and sister hoping for an indication that this might be some kind of joke, but they were both just standing beside the truck with their mouths hanging open. Dad was grinning from ear to ear as he surveyed his investment. Mom was rummaging through the back of our old pickup looking for stuff and barking out orders to my dad. Finally…someone suggested we go on in.

When I opened the creaky old screen door that was hanging by one hinge and looked in at the place for the first time, pretty much all I saw were cobwebs. Why there must'a been hundreds…no thousands…no definitely millions of them. They hung like thick moss from the corners of the ceiling. Everything in the old house seemed to be held in place by those cobwebs. They moved and swayed in the breeze that came in through all the cracks and crevices.

Mom seemed to know just what to do. Soon as we got in the kitchen, she handed out long handled tools—brooms, mops, rakes. Anything long enough to reach up to the ceiling and pull down the old dusty brown webs.

At first I thought those had to be spider webs and I was looking around for the spiders. I mean, with webs that size, those spiders would've had to be the size of my head! Mom promised us kids that they were not from spiders, but our trust was a little bit shaky, after all she and dad had decided to trade in a real house for this old beat up farm! Besides...if there were spiders big as my head, she wasn't going to say so, because she knew if she admitted it out loud...all of us kids would climb right back into the bed of that truck and insist on a ride to greener pastures!

As the first morning wore on we found that the more we tried to remove all those cobwebs, the more it seemed they banded together to protect their territory. It was as if they had formed a little army bent on maintaining their stronghold over the house. Well I was ready for a good battle...no way was I sleeping with these things hanging over my head! I became determined to conquer them and let me tell you, that was not an easy task.

You see, cobwebs are tricky. You can stick a broom up into one of them, and twist it round 'til the web covers the entire whisk...then just when you're ready to pull the web down, it seems to take on a life of its own. It grows and spreads so much that no matter how hard you try, there is always more web still up there.

If you did manage to get one of them off the ceiling then you had another battle on your hands—getting them off your broom. I found out that there's one thing you do not want to do—use a wet broom—if your broom gets wet you just make a big muddy mess right there on the ceiling when you go after the next cobweb and that makes everybody mad. So you better not be dunking your broom in the bucket to clean it off. Instead I would take my broom out in the yard and wipe it through the weeds that grew beside the house, that was better than touching those creepy old webs with my hands.

All morning long we stuck with it. Just when we thought we had a whole room done, we would sit down on the floor and look up at the ceiling, and there would still be more. More cobwebs… more work.

We captured cobwebs most of that first day, moved our stuff into the house, put up the beds and then…well, I guess then we were living there. Everything else was still in boxes stacked up all over the place, but it seems to me that once you sleep and eat…I guess you're an official resident.

Even though no *people* had lived in the house for about 25 years, but that didn't mean it was vacant. Oh no…this house had plenty of other residents.

There was a family of raccoons living in our attic and they were not about to be evicted without a fight. Let me tell you, they put up a good battle, too. Dad got a big old board and nailed it over the place where they were getting in, but by morning they had found another way. He would wait for them to head out for the evening, and then try to be sure he had them "trapped outside" but come morning, they would have worked all through the night to get back into their home. We finally named the little ones Muff and Jeff which made Dad mad. He didn't like for us to name them and get to liken 'em. I guess he thought maybe we were getting sympathetic to their cause.

There was an old red coon dog living in the kitchen. He obviously didn't know he was a coon dog, or we wouldn't have had the problems with the raccoons that lived in our attic. Us kids took to him right away and named him "Alligator Dog" because he never made any noise unless he was about to bite something. He would just lie and wait for his victim…there would be a rush of activity…then he would go back and lie down again. Alligator Dog must have been pretty old when we got him; he was kinda slow, and seemed to groan when he first got up. He had sad eyes and big long ears. Soon as we moved into the house, Alligator Dog moved out to one of the sheds, guess he was hoping for a higher class of roommates. We couldn't get him back in the house, even with bribes of leftover roast. In fact he never did go back in—which made me wonder what the heck we were doing sleeping in there!

The old rickety house had mice everywhere. And there were spiders, big black ones and brown ones, too. We used to put mason jars over them when we found a big one, and after midnight when dad came home from work, he would take care of them. Some nights when he came home there would be ten or twelve mason jars on the kitchen floor and he would have to have them out of there before we were up for breakfast. It was kind of an unspoken rule, we'd catch 'em and he'd kill 'em, and as long as he kept up his end of the deal, we would sleep there one more night.

The squirrels had found a way in too—which wasn't very hard considering three of the windows didn't even have any glass. I still remember the first day Dad put the glass in the front window…one of the squirrels came running down a tree branch…jumped for the house…hit the glass and fell down onto the cellar door. He laid there for a few seconds then got up…inspected the window then ran up and down the window sill…he seemed to be saying "what in the heck is that?" We started calling him "Thunder" 'cause everyday he would come to that window and beat on the glass, like maybe he wasn't sure if it was there to stay. He'd throw nuts at it too, and he never gave up…it went on all summer and fall that first year.

Living at Dunn Movin' Farm was a lot like living in an animal refuge. In the early evening deer would walk right up to the house. They were so unafraid of people that we could get our chairs and sit out under the trees and they would come up so close to us—I think we could've even reached out and petted them.

There was a den of fox living on the edge of the yard (or what appeared to be our 'yard') and we had rabbits living under every brush pile—and there were brush piles everywhere. We used to take ole' Alligator Dog out with us, then jump on the brush piles and make the rabbits run…it was hilarious watching him go crazy trying to decide which one to chase first. Far as I know, he never did catch one, but it sure was fun to watch him chase them until they finally got back under the safety of the dead limbs and branches.

We also had big ole' barn owls out there, and squirrels with webbed-wing legs that could soared from one tree to another. There were rats in the barn lot by the corn crib, and fat old ground hogs that were a heck of a lot meaner than they looked.

Bales of straw had been stacked around the bottom edge of the house...once we got rid of the straw the snakes moved on. The wild animals were a problem sometimes—mostly when we decided they couldn't live in the house anymore—but for the most part, if we kept our distance, they kept theirs.

The creek from the woods ran through the bottom of our yard, and these beautiful flowers with red blooms used to grow right beside the creek bed. I used to go down there and pick the flowers, then turn them upside down and let them float in the water, and I always thought they looked like graceful dancing ladies, just floating on a dance floor there in the morning sunlight.

There was a lot of junk in the yard when we moved in. There were rotten wooden gates, old chairs and rolls of barbed wire all over the yard, as well as tin that had fallen off the barn roofs, broken doors and screens. Big trees that had apparently been hit in lightening storms had fallen from the yard into the gully. To top it all off there was a bunch of stuff you just couldn't put a name to...it seemed that over time people had dumped garbage out our way but with some major elbow grease the old place started to take shape.

The first year we managed to put some decent fences up, get glass in the old windows and put on a new roof. My daddy put a stainless steel sink and some cabinets in the kitchen and he made us an indoor bathroom—complete with running water. You know, these days, we seem to want at least three bathrooms in every house, but in those days, I have to admit we were pretty excited to just get the one.

And before we knew it, it became our place—the place we all grew to love. It was the place we left every morning and returned to every night…the place where knew we'd be safe from the troubles of the world and where we were loved no matter what we had done…the place we called home…our place…Dunn-Movin' Farm.

CHAPTER TWO

THE HOG HOUSE INCIDENT

When we moved onto Dunn-Movin Farm there were a few old beat up hog houses lingering in the orchard. They weren't pretty, but neither was the house we were living in…so I decided to adopt one as my new playhouse.

There were four of the old rustic buildings scattered around between the fruit trees, and after inspecting each one and looking over the views from the holes in the walls, I picked the one that I knew was the special one just for me. It was the only one with a wooden floor…I liked that part a lot.

While everyone else was working to get the old house in some kind of order, I was dragging all of my prized possessions out to my new place. I managed to gather up a blanket, a few toys, a couple of books, a flashlight and an old photograph to hang on the wall of my abode.

As the next few days passed I swept the floors, hung my picture and packed my stuff into my new place. It was just the right size for a seven year old, and far away from the hustle and bustle of the work going on up at the house.

I brought some cookies and lemonade out and settled in. No one seemed to mind I was out there…and I felt like I was in heaven. It just couldn't get much better…I actually was beginning to think that this wasn't such a bad move after all.

The third day after I had "moved-in" to my new retreat, I was enjoying the solitude, reading one of my books, and leaning back on a huge pillow I had swiped from the piles of boxes still waiting to be unpacked when I heard Dad start up the John Deere tractor. I didn't think much of it since I'd heard him start it at least once a day since we moved to the farm and he'd driven it lots of times through the orchard on his way out to the fields. When I heard it coming close to my hiding spot, I crawled way back into my shed…I wasn't sure if he'd like knowing his youngest offspring had taken up residence in a pig sty. So to be on the safe side…I decided to stay out of sight.

The pop of the ole' Deere kept coming closer, but I knew he couldn't see me from his seat behind the wheel. Pretty soon the tractor stopped right next to my special place. I held my ground…and my breath…hoping he wouldn't find me. I heard these strange scraping noises and I could hear him tossing around some old log chains…I just figured he was going to pull down one of the old dead trees near by.

I decided to relax and go back to reading…I didn't even get to the second page of my new book before I knew something was wrong…really wrong! Just as I leaned back onto my pillow…wham…the old hog house gave a groan and with a jerk…it started moving…the tractor seemed to be hijacking my shed! Apparently Dad had hooked a chain onto my new digs and was dragging it off toward the hog pen!

Are you kidding me? I had just gotten this place all cleaned up and now he wants me to abandon ship! I started to scream bloody murder and began to throw stuff out the little hole in the front of the shed. I stood up as best I could and started waving my arms out the hole on the top. Now, I don't know if you've ever been in a hog house when your dad is dragging it across the field, but it is an experience that you won't soon forget. Hog houses don't come with shock absorbers and you will find yourself bouncing from one side to the other and then flopping around like a rag doll...the next thing you know you're upside down and there's a cookie crammed up your nose.

It took awhile for dad to turn around to see how things were going, but when he did he noticed a trail of rather strange looking debris scattered behind my castle. He stopped the tractor...got off...scratched his head and walked back to inspect the pile of childhood litter.

As my once-safe and sound retreat lurched to a halt it sent me rolling out the door and there I was sprawled on the ground just behind my shack...gasping for air.

We had words...lots of them...Dad insisted hog houses were not for little girls but I stood my ground that it wasn't a hog house...it was playhouse. Dad wanted to know what the heck I was doing holed-up in a pig shed and I wanted to know what the heck he was doing trying to hog-tie and steal my new clubhouse.

Finally Mom came out and helped us settle the rift. She said she'd help me pick out a shed from the ones scattered throughout the gully and promised that she'd make me curtains if I would release the hog house in a lady-like manner.

Curtains? I hadn't thought about curtains before! Now I wanted curtains, but I was a shrewd negotiator even at an early age. I told her I would surrender my clubhouse only if she gave me three things...the curtains...an old piece of a tattered rug she'd thrown out of the living room...and the backseat out of the old car someone had tried to bury in one of our ditches alongside the road.

Mom looked over at dad and raised one eyebrow. Dad glanced up the road toward the half-buried car and shrugged his shoulders. He told mom he was having some hogs delivered on Monday and he needed all four sheds. Mom nodded, then told me to start packing up my stuff. Dad said he'd bring down the seat from the abandoned car as soon as he finished moving the hog houses out of the orchard and into the pig pen.

What a deal! Two hours later my new place had a roof, a window and only two holes in the hardwood floors...both of which the rug easily covered. I'd set up shop in the high rent district down in the gully...a great neighborhood... heck the woman (Mom) who lived in the big house on the hill had even brought me warm cookies as a house warming gift...I learned that the most important thing about a home is location, location, location!

I also learned that whenever possible it's best to find a solution where everybody wins. In this case, Dad got his hog house, I got my clubhouse and Mom got rid of the old rug from the living room. The most important thing to remember when you are in the heat of an argument is negotiation, negotiation, negotiation!

CHAPTER
THREE

HOT TIMES

S ummers were hot out at our place, and we had no hope of ever getting air-conditioning. We were lucky to have window fans. Shoot, we were lucky to have windows that opened. Our idea of air=conditioning was to climb up in the bed of the truck and have dad 'n mom take us for a ride. The wind would be blowing our hair, and we would be smiling and sitting up against the cab of the truck, hoping we might stop for some ice cream.

Dad had a way of coming up on a big hill, and then letting off the gas at just the right time, making it feel like you had butterflies in your stomach. We all knew which hills he used for the butterflies, and we would oooooh and ahhhhh each time he pulled his little trick. If our cousins came from town we had to warn them about sitting on the wheel wells, city kids always think that is a good idea until we hit the first big bump in the road, then they turn all white in the face and come crawling up by the cab like the rest of us.

Even without the modern day convenience of air-conditioning, we had our ways to keep cool in the heat of the day. We had those old metal lawn chairs that rocked, and we would sit them in the shade of the elm trees there on the side of the hill where we always had a breeze. We would drink lemonade with big square ice cubes from the freezer.

On really hot days I would "swim" in the horse tank. I never thought about it being gross or nasty. I can remember begging to go out and play in the water, and lots of times I did. The water tank was big enough for me to get under the water and glide from side to side and the water was always so cold it would make you shiver. It wasn't Olympic size by any means, but it sure felt wonderful to me.

There were certain guidelines about dealing with the heat in the dead of the summer. You never should go out wandering in the corn fields on a hot day…the fields were like roasting ovens in the summer time. Maybe that's why we always called corn-on-the-cob 'roastin' ears'. Even the woods could be pretty hot certain times of the summer, but we always knew where the cool parts were and it was always fun to walk through the creek…get your feet wet…then let the mud squish up between your toes.

And the upstairs…let's just say we stayed out of the upstairs during the early afternoons…in my opinion we should have stayed out of there in the evening too. Our bedrooms were as hot in the summer as they were freezing in the winter…in either case it was painful just to breathe.

We even had our own 'pop machine'. Sometimes we'd fill the water tank we used for the livestock with ice we'd made in old ice cream buckets. After the ice was freed from the plastic containers we'd bust it into smaller chunks and dump it into the tank. Then we'd fill the tank with bottles of pop. Each time we'd come back in from the fields, we'd grab an icy-cold bottle…let me tell you…there's nothing like coming in from the field and digging through ice water for a bottle of pop. The only hard part was making sure the animals were all down in the woods so they didn't drink out of the tank and slobber on all our bottles until we were done using it as a cooler.

All of us kids used to try and freeze pop in the big freezer on the back porch. If you timed it just right it was the most fabulous drink in the world…you'd pop-the-top on the bottle so the frozen slush would rise up to the top then you'd hold your mouth over the sweet cool liquid and enjoy the fruit of your finely-timed plan. On the other hand, if you left a bottle in there just a smidgen too long…triumph turned to tragedy…delight to disaster. You'd be left cleanin' out the freezer the rest of the night. Which if you think about it…on a really hot summer night wasn't exactly a bad thing 'cept for how crabby it made my mom. I don't know about your mom…but gettin' my momma really mad…well, if that happened it wasn't going to be a good day for anyone.

I remember one time I left a pop a smidgen too long in the freezer but that time the bottle didn't break…the lid just loosened some so the slush ran down the sides of the bottle onto the metal rack of a shelf, then all over mom's meat packages. Darn…I thought my timing had been perfect but I guess it was just a little off that day, half an hour earlier and I would have had the most exquisite slush.

So there I stood trying to decide the best way to clean up the mess when my brother, Mark, came around the corner. I was about eight years old at the time and he was twice my age. Soon as he saw what had happened he told me I'd better get that mess cleaned up before ma found out or else…Funny thing was that he'd just ruined a Pepsi in the freezer the night before and Mom had told him in no uncertain terms…not to put anymore pop in the freezer because he was going to spoil all her meat.

Now I'm not sure if Mark knew what would happen or if he was trying to help his little sister but...when he told me that I'd be able to savor some of the taste of the pop if I licked it off the shelf to clean it up...I believed him...after all how smart was that? Now you think I'd have known better 'cause Mark was always trying to get me in trouble, but I was pretty gullible. Needless to say I wanted to make sure I got a really good taste so I stuck my tongue way out and gave a good hard lick on the edge of the freezer shelf...and instantly...the freezer and I became one.

Well one of the things that we all learned early on in our family was that when you did something stupid you did not want to draw attention to yourself. It was so much better to figure a way out of your mess before you were discovered. So there I stood...stuck to the freezer shelf...and there was no way that was I going to scream or holler 'cause then my mom would find out what I'd done. And let me tell you...if you'd done something stupid the last thing you'd get from mom was sympathy. So there I stood with the freezer door open trying to figure out how to get the freezer shelf to release my tongue.

I tried to look to either side to see if there was anything I could use to pry my tongue off the shelf. Mark had scooted out the back door as soon as he heard me yelling at him with the freezer shelf stuck to my tongue. I tried to reach over to the counter with my hands, but I couldn't move far enough to reach anything without my tongue jerking me back into place.

19

I happened to have an old shop rag and a pan of water with me 'cause I'd been trying to clean up my mess before Mark came in to 'help'. I was trying to reach the pan and wash rag that I'd placed on the top shelf of the freezer when I heard the screen door slam...uh-oh...I knew I was only moments away from being exposed as an idiot.

Then the miracle happened...just when I reached up to get the rag out of the pan, the pan tipped forward drenching me and everything in the freezer...including my tongue.

Soon as the water hit the cold shelf I was free! What a deal! I had no idea! I rubbed my poor old tongue on the roof of my mouth and decided it still worked. Then I looked out the porch window to see if Mark had witnessed my escape just as Dad rounded the corner. As soon as he saw the frosty air swirling around me he wanted to know what the heck I was doing and why there was water all over the floor. Then he told me to hurry up and shut the freezer door or I'd ruin it and then what would we do.

So I slammed the door shut...bent down and started cleaning up my mess...and I began to think about ways I'd get back at Mark. At the same time, I have to admit, I was wondering which of my cousins would be dumb enough to fall for the same trick. By the time I'd cleaned up my mess I had a mental list of a whole bunch of people I might be able to stick to the freezer shelf...if I could get a pop to overflow without breaking the bottle.

Well...every dastardly plan has its pitfalls. I decided to forget about sticking my cousins to the freezer and concentrate on gettin' back at Mark. I ran out the back door letting the screen slam behind me. I yelled for my mom and told her Mark had a pop that had blown up in the freezer and I thought it had ruined a few of her good roasts. When I rounded the side of the house and started for the gully I heard her holler his name and I could tell she wasn't happy. All I could think is 'Boy is he going to get it!' I skipped a little bit as I headed toward the barn lot, jumped the gate to the orchard and ran for the hills. No need to worry, I knew mom would take care of everything! After all one good turn deserves another.

Yep, most times when you find yourself in trouble, it's better to turn the problem over to a higher authority. I knew who the "higher authority" was at our house, and I knew I could count on mom to get the job done right!

CHAPTER
FOUR

OHHH...
Brother!

You know, I could never figure out why my brother didn't want to hang around with me when we were kids. Now that 40 or 50 years have come and gone, I can look back and see that I'd pestered him everyday of his life until he got old enough to move out on his own.

I followed him everywhere he went…I stole his jeans out of the clean laundry basket and tried to wear them. I'd force myself into his room and watch over his shoulder while he worked on his model cars. Whenever a friend of his stopped over I'd tag along everywhere they went. I knew he didn't like me much…there were times I didn't like him much either…but I'd still follow him all the time anyway. Yep, I'm thinkin' I may have been the primary reason he was so anxious to leave home and get a place of his own.

He tolerated me as long as he could most days. But there were times when he'd just had enough of my attention so he'd try to get away from my watchful eye. He was pretty good at fooling me into 'getting lost'…and like an idiot, I fell for the same trick about a million times over the years.

If Mark and his pals were hanging out in the yard…I was always tailing them and begging to play in whatever game they'd picked for the day. Sometimes they'd be nice for awhile and just try to talk me out of joining them by telling me I'd probably get hurt. That never worked, so then they'd give me the worst job on the team and if I still refused to leave they were forced to come up with another plan that more often than not involved the hay barn.

Here's what they'd do to get rid of me...first they'd send me into the house to retrieve something...then they'd tell me to meet them out at the barn. Well I was always so excited they were going to include me I'd run right up to the house and get whatever they needed. Then I'd run out to the barn as fast as I could, by the time I got there all they guys would be sitting across the barn on top of the neatly stacked bales of hay. They'd just stand there on the far side of the barn...waving for me to come over! Wow! This was going to be great!

I'd climb up to the top of the bales as fast as I could and start walking toward them, all excited to be part of the gang...then WHAM...I'd fall through the bales all the way to the floor. Nice trap...the guys had piled the bales up so that they looked like it a big square block of hay covering the entire floor, but as they'd built-up the stack they'd staggered the bales so that they formed a sort of pyramid that left a huge hole in the right in the center of the stack. Well, as soon as my weight hit that center bale...I'd fall clean through to the the barn floor.

Once I'd fallen, it would take me awhile to drag myself back up to the top of the bales. As I was pulling myself out the boys would take off out to the woods and there was no need to look for them once I got out, 'cause they would be long gone.

The first time this happened it took me some time to figure out how to get back to the top of all those bales. Eventually I figured out that I could pull myself up using the binder twine from the bales over my head. It was hard work, but it was the only way I could get back to the top. Out in our barn nobody could hear you bawling and squalling…and no way I was just going to sit there and wait 'til someone realized I was missing…after all, time passes pretty darn slow when you're stuck in a pit at the bottom of a hay barn.

Once when I had just finished climbing out of my trap Dad came into the barn. He'd sold some hay to a nearby horse farm and needed to start loading up the truck to deliver it. Well I just had to tell him how the boys had tricked me…again…and how I wished I could get back at them. I told him somebody needed to teach them a lesson! Then I told how I would do it I couldn't go down into the woods and find them 'cause they'd told me earlier that afternoon they'd heard a wildcat down there and I was afraid it would catch me and eat me.

Dad just listened to me rant along then he quietly told me there weren't many wildcats in Illinois, least not on people's farms. He said the boys were probably using that as another way to get me to leave them alone. Then he said he suspected they were down at the wide place in the creek skipping rocks…havin' a good laugh 'bout me falling into the hay pit and believing their wildcat tale. With that he simply turned around and went back to loading the hay into the truck.

Hummmmm…so they think I'd believe a dumb old tale like that…did they? Well…I decided right then that I'd teach them not to mess with me! I headed down to the woods toward the wide place in the creek. I wasn't scared of any wildcat anymore "cause my dad always told me the truth and if he said there weren't any...there weren't.

When I reached their hiding place, Mark looked up at me and asked me how I gotten past the wildcats? Then all the boys with him laughed...they sure were having a good time at my expense. Well I was still trying to think of a good answer when something moved in the bushes at the top of the hill behind them. What ever it was made a loud screeching sound...then bushes rustled again.

Okay...my heart started pumpin' and I'm figurin' that maybe dad had it wrong...that sure sounded like a wildcat to me...so I ran lickety-split down the path toward Mark...even if he was mean to me sometimes, I was pretty sure he wouldn't let me be eaten by a wildcat. I guess all the other guys must'a thought the same thing 'cause they moved closer to him too.

We were all standing huddled together on the narrow path between the hillside and the big drop-off that fell into the creek. There was another loud screech and then the bushes above us and the ones in front of us moved at the same time. I swear I saw a wildcat on top of the ridge but I was too scared to make noise...so I just pointed to the brush and everyone looked...we heard sticks cracking and leaves moving...another screech...then we all saw the silhouette of something pacing back and forth.

For a second we all stood frozen...then the silence was broken by shouts of "Let's get out of here!" "I see the wildcats!" "Head for the barn!" All the guys were yelling and running at the same time.

I turned around and started to run up the narrow path as fast as my eight year old legs would take me. Some one yelled "Outta my way...I'm comin' through!" and they knocked me down into the ditch by the creek. I fell over the side and slid down into the shallow water. The mud was so slippery on the edge of the cliff I couldn't climb back up. Every time I attempted I'd just slide right back down to the bottom. Let me tell you I was scared...my heart was pounding and I was crying! All I could do was scream for help. I could see Mark and all of his friends running fast along the path...they were leaving me and my brother was leading the pack!

All of a sudden Mark stopped...hollered at the boys to keep running on the path 'til they got out of the woods. He said it'd take 'em back to the barn and he told 'em to get our dad. Then he turned around and came running back to save me.

He laid down on the ground and held his arm out for me to grab ahold. We could still hear the wildcat's screams as he pulled me out of the ditch and started running together along the narrow path. The cat kept snarling and moving the brush behind us and I could tell Mark was as terrified as I was...but he never left me...he held my hand and pulled me along behind him. By the time we reached the orchard I was too scared to run anymore so he carried me all the way up to the barn on his back.

His friends were already there...panting and heaving...glad to see us make it. Mark put me down on the rack wagon, and we all sat there looking back at the path that led to the woods...waiting to see if the pack of wildcats had followed us.

Everyone started talking at once and it seemed everyone had a different version of what had happened...some of the guys had seen the wildcats...others only heard them....but one thing for sure, we all agreed there was more than one...there had to be at least two...maybe even three. The boys all had different ideas about how and when a wildcat seeks it prey...but we all decided we were lucky to be alive. Mark speculated that the wildcats must've gotten loose from a zoo...someone else they thought they'd heard their parents saying something like that at breakfast.

Just about then mom and dad came walking out of the woods. We all ran toward them telling them about our close call. We told them about the screeching, the bushes, and the wildcats we'd seen on the ridge...how there must've been a whole pack of 'em.

Well instead of sympathy for our scary plight, my folks just burst out laughing. Dad said to the fella's that it wasn't much fun to be tricked or made a fool of...he asked them how it felt to them to be scared out of their wits...then he let out a screech just like the one we heard in the woods. Suddenly we knew how many waildacts were in the pack...two...and they were standing right next to us. We had all fallen for my folks little trick.

Dad said from now on I needed to give Mark and his friends a bit of space, and he told Mark he ought to be a little bit more careful about how he tried to get rid of me in the future. Then he walked up to Mark...patted him on

29

the shoulder and said "Good job, Bud" and let out one more screech.

With that we all had a big laugh.

Afterwards I had a lot more respect for my big brother. I'd always thought he didn't like me much, turned out I was wrong...guess I was precious enough to him that he'd risk his own life to save mine. And when I couldn't run anymore...he'd carried me. It didn't matter that there weren't really wildcats in our woods...he didn't know that at the time...he still came back for me.

People say a man's true character shows in how he handles himself when no one is looking...I don't know about that...but I do know that it shows in how a boy handles himself along a narrow path in the woods when his little sister is stuck in the mud and they're both scared...and I know that Mark's character has always been just fine.

CHAPTER
FIVE

Home
ALONE

My momma was always home when I got off the bus after school. Well, almost always…and it was a good thing, too, 'cause I had a knack for getting myself in trouble whenever the opportunity presented itself.

On the day I want to tell you about, Mom had driven into town to pick up a part for one of the tractors and she didn't make it back before I came home from school.

I was twelve or thirteen…so I was more than old enough to look after myself…at least for a half an hour in the daylight. Well I knew she was going to be late, so I was all prepared…I knew exactly what I was going to do…I'd go into the house…get myself an after school snack and watch the cartoons. Pretty innocent…right? What could possibly go wrong with that plan?

When mom got back she was happy to see me behaving myself. And as soon as she came in the door I pointed out I had no homework to do. I'd changed out of my school clothes and was close to winning a blue ribbon for my behavior. She was proud of me…I know 'cause she said so.

Whatever had happened to the tractor that made her take her trip to town must have been serious because dad was on his way from the shop to fix it and mom said she had things to do before he got home.

So I went back into the living room to watch my cartoons and she went into the kitchen to start dinner. I heard her out there banging pans and going through the refrigerator, but I ignored the sounds and concentrated on watching cartoons. Pretty soon she came in and asked me if I knew what happened to that big bag of prunes in the refrigerator. I told her I hadn't seen any prunes so she left the room. She wasn't gone long before she reappeared in the doorway and announced that she knew she had a bag of prunes in the refrigerator and she wanted to know what happened to them. I shrugged my shoulders and moved closer to the television.

A few minutes passed and I could smell dinner cooking in the kitchen. During a commercial I wandered in to see what we were having. Mom was on the back porch with everything out of the refrigerator stacked on the floor. She was wiping down the shelves and she asked me again if I had seen anyone take that bag of prunes.

I was pretty tired of hearing about the missing fruit. First of all I had no idea what a "prune" looked like, I hadn't seen anything unusual in the fridge and I had already told her about a billion times I didn't know anything about the prune mystery.

She took offense at my little speech about the prunes, and went on to say that *someone* knew where they were, after all, they wouldn't just grow legs and walk away!

I just shrugged my shoulders and went back into the living room and settled in to watch the rest of my show.

As soon as mom finished cleaning out the refrigerator there was a rush of activity out on the porch where we kept a bucket we filled with trash. Then she came stomping into the living room with her evidence...she thrust the empty prune bag onto the floor in front of me and said in a loud and commanding voice, "Here is the empty bag...now you *must* know what happened to those prunes!"

I looked at the sack and turned it over, and there on the front was a little picture of the fruit. "OH...you mean them *big* raisins!" I said. "I ate the whole bag for my after school snack!"

If she had told me she was looking for raisins earlier I have told her right away that I'd eaten them. Shoot, I just thought there were big fat, juicy, good raisins in that bag! They were huge...just like the ones in the picture on the front of the package.

Now the tone of my mother's voice changed from anger to one of concern. "You ate this entire bag of prunes?"

"Yea. Raisins...prunes...what's the difference? "

"Well" said mom, "You're about to find out."

Turns out there is quite a big difference...for the next two days I became well acquainted with the benefits...and detriments...of eating an entire bag of prunes, and to this day I can't stand the sight of them!

From that point on I became pretty careful 'bout what I stuck in my mouth, and pretty cagey about fruit in general. As far as I'm concerned there are a whole lot of things in life where a-little-dab'll-do-ya...remember to add prunes to that list.

CHAPTER
SIX

DAD 'n

His Jam

My dad loved jams and jellies. He was a real jelly connoisseur...and my mom...well she was the queen of making jelly. We had jelly from every fruit she could get her hands on...blackberry jelly...raspberry jam...peach, strawberry, pear, gooseberry, apple butter and one time we even had some persimmon jelly...and that's saying somethin'.

We kept a whole cupboard full of all the colorful jars of jams and jellies right in our kitchen. And mom was one of the original recyclers...soon as you had an empty jar, you washed it out and put it in the sink...pretty soon mom would scald it and next thing you'd know it'd be filled with some bright colored jelly and have a paraffin lid melted over the top to keep it safe.

Every morning when I was gettin' ready for school, dad would be getting up too. See...all dad needed was about his six hours of sleep after his regular job...then he'd be up and ready to head out to do his chores on the farm. He always had the same routine...first he'd drag himself outta bed...pour himself a big old cup of coffee and turn on the radio to a news channel. Then he'd settle in at his spot at the head of the table and start dumping ten or twenty spoons of sugar into his cup...there'd be little mountains of sugar spilt all around his cup from where he'd miss and by the end of his breakfast there'd be coffee rings all over that end of the table.

Spread all around him was the newspaper, his ashtray and and a platter of toast with a big jar of jelly and a butter knife. The toaster always sat there on the table next to him with the cord stretching clear over to the wall.

Sometimes there'd be some eggs and ham left over from our breakfast, and he'd add that to his platter of toast 'n jelly, but if we'd eaten it all, he didn't seem to mind much…long as we left him at least six slices of bread for his toast. The heels of the bread didn't count…you had to leave about half the loaf of the real bread else there was going to be some serious trouble.

The morning I want to tell you about started out with my mom fighting with my hair…now if you'd read my first book you'd know this was an ongoing battle…my mom and my hair. She still to this day comments on my hair and threatens to give it a good brushing every time I see her.

Anyway…Mom and I were in the living room…she'd already wet my hair down and she was using a big old stiff brush…trying to make it lay down. She had just finished saying that my hair had the same consistency as a horse tail…well that seemed to give her an idea…so she produced a big old thick brown rubber band and pulled my hair back tight…giving me one of those 1960's facelifts…you know the one where your ponytail is so tight you can't blink your eyes. Anyway, she was grunting and groaning and trying to hold my hair tight while she got the rubber band off her wrist. She was saying all sorts of things under her breath which I better not repeat here, and she was hinting that if she couldn't get it up and out of my face she just might give me another hair cut. You see mom was always telling everyone to 'get that hair outta your face!' It didn't matter if you had to shave your head…as far as she was concerned …so be it. About that time we heard the toaster pop up for the first time…

"Jean," Dad said, "This new jelly of yours has gone rancid…I don't think we should be eating this stuff".

Mom never missed a beat…she didn't let loose of my hair either.

"If you don't like that jelly, get yourself a different kind outta the cupboard," was all she said.

Pulling my hair even tighter…she wound the rubber band around my hair one more time and pulled it…tight. And me…well I just wanted to get this over with and be on my way before she made a permanent bald spot on the back of my head. Just then the toaster popped again…

"What the heck kinda jelly have you got out here?" Dad wanted to know. He made a gagging and spitting sound and said that was the worst jelly he had ever tasted and that he didn't think it was fit to feed the hogs. He said it didn't have any sugar in it, and it burned when he swallowed it.

My mom gave him directions to the jelly cupboard and told him to quit bellyaching and go get himself some jelly he liked. She wet the comb…ran it through my bangs…gave my ponytail a great big yank to be sure it was still connected…then shoved me toward the door. That was her way of telling me that she'd done her best and was finished with the battle for the day. Just then the toaster made its familiar sound one more time…

Now dad was spitting and gagging as he made an all-points bulletin announcement…

"You're going to kill someone with this stuff. I can't eat any of it. You KNOW I can't start my day on an empty stomach. I'm going to have to go out and get in the truck and drive up to the grocery store just to buy some decent jelly." Whew...guess he'd gotten *that* off his chest.

Well, those were fightin' words around our place. Mom let out a heavy sigh and headed toward the kitchen. When she walked in and took in the scene at the table...she saw dad sitting in his usual spot....a big ole' white platter of toast right in front of him with about six pieces of uneaten toast...each one missing a single bite. There was a plate of butter and jar of jelly with a butter knife on top just to his left...it had toast crumbs spilt in the top and some butter on the rim of the jar.

"Is that what you've been eating?" Mom demanded.

Dad looks up from his paper...studies her face and informed her that she'd lost her touch when it comes to making jelly. He said he wasn't going to complain when the persimmon jelly wasn't good, but this pink stuff is the worst stuff he'd ever tasted. He said she'd better dump what she's got in the cupboard and start over. He said he'd be embarrassed to even try and pass any of that stuff off onto the relatives. He said it is a big waste of money to be making jelly we can't even choke down. He said in town they had good jelly at the store, and he just might start buying it to save us from the horrible stuff she had turned out in her last batch. I think he even banged his fist on the table a couple of times.

Well I knew better than to get in the middle of that discussion so I stayed in the doorway...I could tell a storm might be brewing and I didn't want to get caught up in the funnel cloud.

Mom repeated her question a little louder and this time she pointed at the vat of jelly in front of him to make sure he understood what she was talking about.

Finally dad gets the drift, and began to realize it was one of *those* questions...the kind where you better be careful how you answer...so he looked over the table, figured he might be in trouble...coughed once...cleared his throat and said he hadn't eaten any of *that* jelly.

"Good thing" Mom said. "That's the hair gel I used on Doris' hair".

Poor old Dad, always sticking his foot in his mouth, and apparently, sometimes he'd use a little hair gel to wash it down.

CHAPTER
SEVEN

RUNNIN'
IN THE
RAIN

I was the last one picked up by the bus in the morning and the first one dropped off at night. Lots of times I'd get tired of waiting for the bus in the morning so I'd just walk on to school, and sometimes the bus driver got tired of waiting for me when school was out, so I'd have to walk home after school, too.

Well I walked home from school a lot when I was a kid and there were some rules you had to follow...don't get in a stranger's car...don't walk through any mud puddles you don't have to...stay over on the shoulder of the blacktop and walk against the traffic and most importantly make sure you got home before dark. Other than that...everything else was fair game.

Out in our little town when you got to the fifth grade they moved you up into the high school building and we had class up on the top floor. That year when they had the first football game of the season, I was all excited and asked if I could stay and watch...mom wasn't too keen on the idea...'cause we only had one truck that was runnin' and dad would have to take it to work, so that meant I'd have to walk home as it was getting dark. Well, after I'd missed the first three or four games and after I'd resorted to lots of begging and pleading...I finally wore her down and she agreed to let me go as long as I did two things...one, I had to call her from the phone booth on the Main Street of town before I started for home, and two, I had to start for home before it was dark.

I remember that night, I was so excited to be going to the game even though I didn't have anyone to sit with…and I wandered around the bleachers for a long while. Well, with all the lights on around the football field, I didn't notice how dark it was getting until the game was almost over. I made my way to the phone booth and called home. I told my momma I was starting out and began my infamous journey…

Walking the first few blocks was no big deal, there were lots of street lights and I knew several of the kids I saw walking toward their houses. But as I rounded the last corner in town and made it to the first farm along the road it dawned on me how dark it was out this way. And to top it off it was starting to rain…every once in awhile a big clap of thunder would sound, and I could see lightning off in the distance.

I picked up my pace…

About that time some old fella…probably about forty years old…stopped and offered me a ride. He looked pretty scary to me so I declined and started walking a little faster…I only had a little over a mile to go.

The guy must have felt sorry for me and turned around and came back for another try. He said he was pretty sure I was gonna get soaked before I got home if I walked. He said he knew my daddy and he called him by name, but I was pretty sure I'd never seen this guy before in my life so I declined again…crossed over to the other side of the road and started to run a little bit.

Well let me tell you, it was dark out…really dark, and when the taillights of the guy's car faded over the hill I started feeling pretty alone and pretty scared. I'm not exactly sure what I was scared of, but that didn't matter, my adrenaline was kickin' in...

I kept trotting along and I was getting close to Crossin's farm...that place was scary even in the daylight. I was pretty sure Frankenstein lived there, and some of the town folk had repeated rumors of how old man Crossin had fed some kid he didn't like to his hogs. I stepped up my pace again...I wanted to get past that place as quickly as I could.

Just as I started running again I heard something rustlin' about in the bushes down in the ditch...my heart started pumpin even faster and I let out a whoop...I knew I'd better high tail it home as fast as my skinny little legs could carry me before something bad happened.

Just then a big old black cloud opened up and dumped buckets of rain on me...I started runnin' flat out. I was running as hard as I could and watching the ground so I could see the edge of the road to guide me. All of a sudden there was a huge clap of thunder and a lightning bolt lit up the spooky old Crossin farm. That was enough for me...I threw my sweater into the ditch and started screaming and running for all I was worth.

I was almost to the halfway mark...still screaming and running when something passed me. I figured it must'a been a dog, 'cause I could hear it panting and I could hear it's feet hitting the gravel...but there was no way I was going to slow down to check it out.... I just kept hollering and running like my tail was on fire.

That's when it happened...

I ran flat faced into a person! Someone else was out there...the Boogie Man! Now what should I do? Well I hauled off and hit 'em as hard as I could...he fell backwards down on the ground in front of me, and made an "ugh" sound. Then I jumped up on his chest and stomped my feet...screaming "help! Help! HELP!"

Well I don't know who I thought was going to help...'cause there was no one out there but me and the Boogie Man that I was tromping into the ground. The guy was trying to get up off the ground, so decided I'd better defend myself...I jumped on his back and began to beat him about the head and shoulders. I wrapped my arms around his neck and pulled back as hard as I could, screaming at the top of my lungs all the while!

Somewhere...seemed like in the distance...I could hear someone trying to say something...well it dawned on me the guy was saying something...what the heck was he was trying to say? My name? MY NAME! He was trying to say my name! I stopped screaming...but still hung onto his back...choking him by the neck. He kept trying to croak out a few words. There was a flashlight lying on the ground not far from us and in the dim light I could make out the size of the person...he wasn't much bigger than me!

Once more he choked out the word; "do-ris!"

Ummmm...I think I know that voice...wait a minute; something about this guy was familiar. Even though he sounded funny...like he was having trouble getting his breath...it was a voice I knew...uh, oh...I let loose of his neck...

"Doris! What's the dickens is the matter with you! Get off my back!" He bent over, picked up his flashlight and smacked it against his leg. The beam got brighter and I could see more of him now.

Hey! It wasn't a guy after all! It was...a woman! It was...my mom!

She'd been worried about me walking home from town in the dark, and had started walking toward me as soon as I had called home. The dog that had passed me was our dog...I was just too scared to recognize her. Soon as I realized it was my momma, all of my courage drained away and I started to cry. After I got all the bawling out of my system we walked back to our place together. Me 'n my mom 'n our dog. We didn't say much. Guess we didn't have too. She knew I was too scared to make that trip alone in the dark again, and I knew it too.

Once we got in the house, we washed off our scrapes and bruises, picked the gravel out of our cuts and had a good laugh about it all. In fact, we had ourselves a good old fashioned giggle fit. Then we wrapped ourselves up in blankets...made some hot chocolate and kept talking about it 'til the wee hours of the morning. Mom kept saying she had no idea I could jump that high or hit that hard. Every time we tried to stop talking about it, one of us would burst out laughing, snort the cocoa out our nose and then it would start all over again! When Dad came home from work we told him about it, too.

Dad said fear is an awesome motivator; it can make you do some pretty weird stuff. Fear can make something big

46

and scary out of nothing at all…well, I guess he was right, but he forgot to mention how a little beam of light, the presence of a person you love, and a little bit of laughter can make everything safe and warm again.

CHAPTER
EIGHT

HISTORY
Repeats Itself...

Back home it seemed like every Sunday all the aunts, uncles and cousins would descend on our place like locusts. Mom would fry chicken all morning...make pounds of potato salad...dozens of roastin'-ears and giant fruit cobblers then these folks would come and pick the platters clean.

Once we'd eaten everything in sight, us kids would all wander out to the big hayfield behind the barn lot and strike up a game of baseball. I was the youngest in the bunch...ten...I was the only girl and to top it off I was left-handed...so no one really wanted me to play. Because of my supposed handicaps, and the fact no one else liked playing the position...I always had to be the catcher.

My big brother, who could fire a ball like it was shot from a cannon, was usually the pitcher. He didn't believe in cutting me any slack because I was a girl or because of my age or the left-handed thing...in fact, he thought if he threw hard enough to knock me over a few times, maybe I'd give up and go in the house.

One afternoon after we'd all consumed the buffet fit for a small army, Mark and about ten cousins and I headed off to play a friendly game of baseball while the women cleaned up the mess we'd left in the kitchen.

Mark pitched a few balls to warm up, and offered me the option of going back in the house. I was pretty sure I could hold my own with the big boys so I declined.

One of my older cousins and Mark were always trying to prove which one was the better baseball player. Well, when he came up to bat Mark tried again to get someone else to catch besides me, but I wasn't about to loose my place on the field. He shook his head at me…made a face that said he wanted me to leave…then wound up and fired off one of his infamous fast balls. I don't know exactly what happened, but the next thing I knew I was in the living room on the couch with an ice pack on my head. I ended up with a goose egg just above my eyebrow, and I didn't have to do my chores for a week…that was it for me…I didn't play any team sports for the next 25 years.

In fact the next time I played ball I was 35…married and had children. Well, I only had to be on the field about an hour before history repeated itself…

At the shop where my husband worked they'd decided to gather up all the old decrepit softball players and play one more tournament for old times sake. The game was going to be on the Fourth of July. All the old geezers dug out their gloves…practiced a few times…and then day before the big game one of them read the fine print on the form which stated that for every man on the team they had to have a woman. Well that was a bit of a problem…they scoured the shop and came up with two women who'd played softball in college, so they decided all the other guys had to bring their wives to fill in the gaps. And that, my friend, is how I got drug back into the game.

It was game day and we only had about an hour to practice with the guys before the big event started. First they stuck me out in right field, but when the ball came my way and I and yelled at my husband, "What am I suppose to do"… the men on the team just shook their heads and started to make suggestions on what position I should play. You guessed it…at 35 I was still the youngest one on the team,…I was still left-handed and to top it off now I was fat and out-of-shape…so after a rather heated discussion they formed a huddle to decide where to put me next.

I'd made it clear I didn't want to play, but the rules said every team member had to play at least one inning. The only exceptions were for injuries, or for the pitcher…the pitcher could be taken out anytime and replaced with another player…hmmmm…after careful consideration the all guys approached me as a unified front…they explained if I pitched just one ball…one ball…then they could replace me on the mound and I could sit under a shade tree and drink sweet tea the rest of the afternoon.

Well that sounded pretty good to me, so I agreed.

I walked out to the pitcher's mound all dressed up in my new jersey and holding the fancy left-handed glove we had grabbed at Farm 'n Fleet on the way to the game. The umpire announced we should "play ball." A little scrawny guy walked up to the batters box and hit his shoes with the bat. I chuckled and thought "what a showoff."

The catcher nodded at me and I pitched my first…and last ball. Turns out that skinny kid was an all-star player off some college team. He hit a line drive…so hard I never saw it until it got about six inches from my face. Believe it or not I actually leaned toward it and thought "What the heck is that thing?"

You know that cracking noise two croquet balls make when they click together? Well, I remember hearing that sound… I remember my husband, Marc, who was playing third base, screaming my name…I remember turning to look at the first baseman…I felt myself hit the ground like a sack of potatoes…

My eyes slammed shut and I couldn't open 'em…I felt Marc grab my head in his hands and heard him say "Honey…are you okay? I think you've lost your eye!"

I said, "Do I look like I'm okay? And it's not my eye, it's my nose, 'cause I can't breathe!"

This man I married who is sweet and kind, and so soft-hearted our kids called him "Marshmallow Dad" began to scream and swear like a sailor. He jumped up…ran frantically in a circle…ripped the sweat pants of a girl who had been playing shortstop…and immediately began to wrap them around my face. Now remember, it's the Fourth of July in Iowa…it's about 110 degrees in the shade…my nose is inverted…I'm having trouble breathing, and Marc's trying to suffocate me with someone else's sweatpants. I am *not* having a good day.

By this time I couldn't talk anymore, but I heard everything that was going on around me. Someone had called an ambulance…I could hear the faint sounds of the siren far-off in the distance…I was sure they wouldn't make it in time. Everyone on the field was talking at the same time and they sounded pretty worried.

When the ambulance finally pulled up, some woman jumped out and started talking to my husband. She declared that she'd never seen anything like this before. I laid there and thought "Okay, I'm hurt…and I'm hurt bad this time..." She rattled off some instructions to other people and then started talking to me in a really loud voice. My head was hurtin' and I just wanted to tell her quiet down...after all, I could hear, I just couldn't talk.

Finally, she produced a stretcher about four inches wide...it took six big guys to lift me onto that toothpick, then they had to precariously balance me as the heaved me into the ambulance.

When we got in the emergency room I heard Marc talking to doctors who were trying to explain my options. They said they could put about 45 stitches in my face...or...they had this new product, kind of like body super glue they could use that and it probably wouldn't even leave much of a scar.

Marc was taking his sweet time thinking it over. I mustered up all the courage I had left and yelled out "Just glue it!"

The fact that I was speaking again seemed to thrill everyone in the room, and I managed to get one eye open. It seemed like I was looking out of a tunnel, and it felt like my forehead was swollen and sticking out past the end of my nose.

After they'd glued my face back on, the doctor said he wanted to talk to me in private. A little short nurse in a blue uniform came and escorted my husband out of the room...then the doctor put on a clean white coat...sat down on one of those three legged chairs and wheeled it right up close to my face. I was hoping he was going to tell me why I could only get my one eye to open.

Instead, he got so close to me I could hardly focus on his face, then he said firmly but quietly, "Now, you must be honest with me! You have to tell me if your husband has done this to you!"

I was flabbergasted! I opened my one good eye wide and said, "What do you think he did? Popped me in the nose in front of 200 people, drug me out to a pitcher's mound and then welded a softball to my face? "

Oh I forgot to mention that the ball was still there when the paramedic came...marshmallow man couldn't bear to touch it!

Remember that song..."it's one, two, three strikes you're out..." Well, I used to think you weren't out until the third strike, but apparently I had that part wrong...I was out before even one strike was thrown.

Guess I've finally learned my lesson...I do *not* belong on the ball field and the team must have thought so too, because they've never asked me to play again.

CHAPTER
NINE

CHEERS!

I wanted to be a cheerleader all the years I attended school. I wanted it in the worst way. Unfortunately for me, other girls at our school wanted to be cheerleaders too, and they had more talent and experience in that arena than I did.

Now my junior year I decided to stalk some of the cheerleaders and see what they had that I didn't have. Turned out they had a bunch of assets I was missing.

In the first place they had great hair that always looked neat and softly curled around their face. My hair was stick straight and had the consistency of a horse tail. It was always scraggly and my bangs were usually uneven. Hard as I tried, my hair never looked neat and it was only curly if my mom gave me one of those poodle perms…even then it was more like a twisted bunch of knotted twine than curls. If I put rollers in my hair and slept in them all night, as soon as I took them out and ran a brush through my curly locks they immediately went limp and straight again. To add to the challenge I had a cowlick right over my widow's peak…I have this thick bunch of hair on the very top of my head that grows forward and falls onto my forehead. Guess you could say there's not much hope for me ever having good hair.

Besides great hair, the cheerleaders I was scoping out didn't have bruises all over their legs. I, on the other hand, had bruises and scrapes on my legs every day of my life. I was always runnin' into something that left a big ole' bruise somewhere. I had red ones, purple ones, blue ones, green ones and yellow ones. My legs looked like a full color world map…some bruises might take on the shape of India or Alaska and others might merge together so they looked like the whole Pacific Ocean. And I had scratches all over me too. You'd have thought I went home nights and fought with wildcats. Instead they came from hay bales and running through the brambles in the woods. Guess my legs weren't exactly cheerleader smooth and silky.

Back then the cheerleaders had white knee socks that stayed up all day. I didn't even own a pair of knee socks and even if I could have gotten knee socks and glued them to my legs so they would stay up…they never would've covered up all my war wounds. All I ever wore were anklets and they were always working their way down into my shoes. We had a dirt road, and it seemed that most of the dirt ended up on my socks during my morning hike to the bus. They were white when I left home in the morning, but by the time I got to school they always looked like someone had been wearing them for at least a week. It was beginning to look even more like I was just not cheerleader material.

I also noticed our cheerleaders had great smiles. I didn't have a great smile…I had false teeth with a crooked tooth right in the front…why the dentist thought they'd look more real with a crooked tooth is beyond me…they were straight before my horse kicked 'em outta my mouth…but that's another story. Besides, everyone in my school knew I'd spit my false teeth into some fat lady's lap at the movie house, and there just was no living that down. Yup…I definitely was thinking that my chances of becoming a cheerleader were pretty slim.

A couple more things the cheerleaders at our school could do were the splits and flip-flops. I could kinda do the splits, and I figured if I learned to do back flips I just might be a shoo-in for the squad. So I worked all summer in our front yard learning to throw myself over backwards...a few times I even landed on my feet. Come tryout time at the end of August I'd almost mastered the task...about fifty percent of the time I'd land in an upright position. But the learning curve had upped my bruise ratio and I looked more war-torn than ever.

And last but not least, I realized that all the cheerleaders in our school were popular...which is pretty much the main reason I wanted to be a cheerleader in the first place. I thought the girls were popular because they were cheerleaders...it never dawned on me that being popular was one of reasons they made the squad in the first place.

After trying and failing three years in a row I finally decided to settle for level two...the pom-pom squad. I know the pom-pom squad really isn't level two...but it was for me at the time because I *really* wanted to be a cheerleader.

Becoming a pom-pom girl meant spending most of the summer learning a group routine with everyone who was in the competition...then I had to find a few girls to form a smaller bunch so we could make up a new routine all our own. First I tried to get in with some of the experienced girls, but no one would have me. I was pretty sure the reason they didn't want me in their group was that they were just a bunch of stuck up snobs...it never dawned on me that it had anything to do with the fact I was awkward looking...couldn't stay with the beat of the music and had a tendency to throw the pom-pom about twenty feet each time I raised my arms.

So I decided I didn't want to be part of their old group anyway...I'd find my own group of girls that were same as me...high hopes...no experience and determined. We put our heads together...picked a song and I played it at full volume all day...everyday...all summer long. We worked together to create the perfect routine...we formed circles, rectangles and triangles...we stomped and beat our pom-poms together to make clapping sounds...we bowed eloquently and jumped as high as we could...Dad always said "practice makes permanent" so I wanted to be sure we practiced every possible moment. We practiced in the yard...in the barn...in the gully...we practiced rain or shine...'til we knew the routine backward and forward. Our dance started to take shape...we had our tango down to a science and things were looking up. I was sure we would be the best of the show!

Finally the big day came to present our routine to the world. We had matching outfits, color-coded to make us look fabulous. My troop of eight was ready to take on all the other squads. What we lacked in experience I figured we'd make up for with pure enthusiasm and our desire to be part of the popular crowd. We had a plan...we had our original routine...we had matching outfits and we were going to move up in the world together!

At the beginning of tryouts the judges handed out numbered panels that we were supposed to safety pin on our shirts. My number was thirteen…lucky thirteen. Oh well, I wasn't going to let a little thing like an unlucky number ruin my turn…after all, I was confident I could make the squad. What could go wrong? I had practiced…I had worked hard and I was ready to strut my stuff! This would be my moment of glory! I was going to make it this time…I just knew it!

I even thought I looked good that day…I'd curled my hair that morning…then sprayed it with a shellac-like hairspray…I'd put rubber bands around my legs to keep my brand new white knee socks in place…I'd put makeup on my bruises so you couldn't see them very well from a distance…I'd squirted on some of my mom's perfume and I'd brushed my teeth and glued them in. I was prepared to take my place in the winner's circle!

When tryouts began we all did the big group routine first. I felt like I'd held my own in that part so my confidence was growing. I'd kept my arms straight, but not too stiff…I'd smiled the entire time and I had not moved my lips when I counted out the beats of the music. Never once did I accidently throw a pom-pom even though my hands were sweaty. Yup…I was pretty sure I'd not made a single mistake.

Next we broke out into our smaller groups…when I gathered my little flock around me I could tell they needed to have their confidence built back up. A few of them were a little shaken after the first routine…one girl in particular…but I worked hard to convince them that we would really "wow" the judges with our finale!

Time drug it's feet until they finally announced it was our turn…we were the last group to perform. There were only five judges, all of them teachers from our school. I knew that one of them didn't like me very much…I'd thrown up on her desk when I was in the sixth grade and I didn't think she'd forgiven me yet. That made me a little nervous…after all it's never good to have an enemy in the judges' chair. But, what could I do? The show must go on. I figured if I got the votes of the other four judges…I'd still make it!

Our group marched out to the center of the gym holding our pom-poms at our hips. We formed a circle and the music began to play. So far so good! Then the weird stuff started…the first time I raised my arms over my head my number fell off my shirt and floated to the floor…but I didn't let that bother me…I just looked those judges straight in the eyes and smiled. Nothing was going to ruin this moment for me!

In my head I counted out the first 16 beats from the song…we were then supposed to move out of the circle formation and make a rectangle. Apparently no one else in my troop had taken geometry, because they were forming some other type of shape…maybe the hind leg of a dog I was thinking. So I stopped moving forward and started going backward…thinking that if I got to the other side of the formation…over by the paw of the dog leg…we'd look more like a shape the judges might recognize…maybe something kinda like an octagon.

That's when one of the girls started screaming at me… dropped her pom-poms…plopped down on the floor and started bawling. She just sat right down in the middle of our little group and refused to budge...blubbering like a baby. I tried to step over her to get back into a line. It was right about then that the rubber band that was holding up one of my socks snapped and shot off my leg and hit her smack in the forehead...well...that started her making a racket that would've make a dog run for cover. With all of her noise it was hard to hear our music, so we missed a few beats of our routine and it wasn't long after that when our whole dance just fell apart.

Our arms were up when they should've been down...some girls were trying to make a square instead of lines...half of us were marching and the other half was standing still...then all the other girls started bickering right there in the middle of the song. It was mutiny! I was the only one still trying to finish the routine...the whole army had turned on itself...we were doomed! But...I wasn't about to give up...this was my last shot, I just had to keep trying!

So I did...I just had to keep on keeping on...right there in the middle of World War III. I kept prancing around, arms up...two-three-four; arms out...two-three-four; arms down...two-three-four, determined to finish.

Finally just as the song was about to end...one of the girls in our group hauled off and smacked one of the others in the face. This made the girl sitting on the floor start to kick her feet and wale even louder. Then someone threw a pom-pom...it landed on top of my head and stuck there. I just pretended not to notice...I kept sashaying around, arms up…two-three-four; arms out…two-three-four; arms down…two-three-four and…ta-dah…I bowed.

When the music stopped I put my pom-poms on my hips and marched to the sidelines…with my head held high and a smile plastered on my face. I was still wearing my purple and gold "pom-pom" hat. The rest of the bunch was standing in the middle of the gym screaming and crying; unaware the whole event was behind us. I'd done it…I'd finished the whole song but I have to admit that was the longest three minutes and sixteen seconds of my entire life.

The judges told us to take our seats on the other side of the gym with the other girls…the respectable contestants. After a few whispers from the judges table one of them came over and told everyone they would call the winners and post a list of the chosen squad in two hours on the outside gym doors. Then they asked all the contestants to leave.

I lingered in the locker room hall for quite a while…I could hear the judges muted voices and then I heard everyone break-out laughing. I was pretty sure I knew what they were laughing about, so I decided to just head home…I made my way out through the double doors into the afternoon sun.

I walked across the street to the little store…ordered up a chocolate malt from the ice cream counter and snuck around the side of the building to drown my sorrows. I sat down in the shade of the building and let the water works begin to flow…no sense waiting around for the list this time…I knew I didn't have a chance!

Once I had cried it all out, I started walking home...defeated...my shoulders sagged...my feet were dragging...I was at the lowest point of my life. I'd blown my last chance...I was never going to be 'one of them'...I was a loser in a big way.

When I reached our lane and started up the hill I could see my mom and someone else sitting out in the yard talking. We must have company I thought dejectedly... great...just what I needed to top off my day. Well it turned out to be my oldest sister and her family had come out to visit. Soon as I got within hearing distance Becky shouted out "How'd it go?" Mom must have told her what I was up to.

"Okay" I said...no reason to air my dirty laundry to her. I bet she never had anything like this happen anyway. Seemed like everything she touched turned to gold. I glanced down at the ground and made my way into the house...up the stairs and into my room. I yanked my copy of the song off my record player...snapped it in half and threw it in the garbage. I never wanted to hear that song again!

I laid down on my bed with the fan blowing in my face and cried a little more...then drifted off to sleep.

I thought I heard the phone ringing when I woke up, but decided it must have been a dream. Then I heard my mother's voice...she called to me to come down...I had a phone call. I figured it was probably someone calling to rub in the fact I'd made a fool of myself that afternoon.

I dragged myself down the stairs and picked up the receiver...a voice on the other end identified itself as my old sixth grade teacher. Great...the one judge I knew voted against me before I even walked out on the court!

She asked how I was and then she told me that she wanted to be the first to congratulate me on my ability to keep my head in the midst of so much confusion. What was this all about? Some new way to humiliate me? Well, good...I was glad someone was having a good time at my expense! Guess she won the coin toss and was going to be the one to tell me everything I had done wrong.

I had to admit...she sure sounded pleasant, even nice, as she delivered her dreaded news. I thought how much nicer she seemed on the telephone then she did in person. She continued telling me how impressed she was by my performance...how she was the new pom-pom coach for fall and how she wanted to welcome me to the squad.

Welcome me to the squad? Was she kidding? This must be some kind of joke! I asked her if I could call her back. Then I looked up her phone number from the phone book...I just had to be sure no one was pulling my leg. Well guess what...she answered the phone and verified I was on the squad!

Whew hew! What a lucky break! Maybe they had me mixed up with someone else. Maybe they thought I was number was 31! It didn't matter to me how it happened, I was in! In that one moment I went from being the biggest loser in history, to having the world on a string!

Mom 'n Dad must have told us a million times, "It was better to do something...even if we did it wrong...than to just stand there like a bump on a log and do nothing."

Much as I hated to admit it, they were right again. I knew the whole time I was doing my routine…it was all going wrong…but at the same time I knew that I was going to do something…I wasn't going to just stand there and do nothing. In the end, my doing "something" paid off for me…in a really big way.

CHAPTER
TEN

THE FOG
'n
THE Pole Light

Pert' near every farm in the Midwest has a pole light. Ours was big and bright and in the middle of the barn lot and you could see it from anywhere on the farm. It was lit twenty-four hours a day...we never turned off that pole light...we even left it on if we were gone on vacation...that way we figured most people would think we were home.

Turning off the pole light was a big deal...you had to crawl behind the freezer...stretch your arm to its full potential...reach your longest finger all the way out 'til your face was smashed against the wall...then try to give the switch one good flick without getting electrocuted.

The night I want to share with you, the pole light was on.

Our neighbors that lived clear down the lane from us, past our woods and over the biggest hill to the back of farm...the preacher and his wife, had just called to tell us our horses were out in their field.

This was not good news 'cause there was a fog rollin' in, but Mom and I figured if we hustled down to the edge of the woods...jumped the fence and came up through their place, we'd be able to shoo the horses back onto our land through the gate before nightfall. Then once we got 'em on our property, we could let 'em back in our woods down by the creek. Because we both knew the woods well we were not at all worried 'bout getting lost coming home after dark, so we grabbed one weak...almost dead...flashlight and headed out across the fields. Dad had a cold he stayed up at the house but that was okay, we knew we could do the job without him.

About an hour later we were feeling pretty good. We had no problem finding the horses and getting them back on our place, and as we put the last of the three through the gate we both remarked on how thick the fog was getting. As we started back up to the house through the woods our flashlight died and by now the valleys were full of a dense fog, so we were really having trouble making out exactly where we were. We started walking a little quicker up the hill toward the fence so we could crawl over into one of our fields. Mom kept reminding me to keep the pole light in sight as a guiding point. We were talking about how the sailors used lighthouses, and laughing about having our own kind of "lighthouse" in the barn lot. The pole light seemed to have moved to our left, so we changed course to move back in line with it. The fog was even thicker now...so thick we couldn't even see each other even though we were only a few feet apart.

Finally, we stumbled upon the fencerow and crawled over it...into what had to be our bean field. It sure felt like we'd been walking forever. Wait...we couldn't be in the bean field 'cause there were trees...we must be in the orchard. We figured we might've been walking parallel to the fence...maybe that's why it seemed like the light had moved. From time to time mom and I would shout our location back and forth as we picked our way along the fence. Man...it seemed to be a long way back...must be 'cause of the fog that it seemed so far. Still...we could see our guiding light...a small comfort beam surrounded by the fog...so we kept moving forward.

It wasn't long before Mom started making a lot of strange noises. Seemed she had stepped in the creek and it was deeper than she expected…almost knee high and that was unusual for our creek. Only after a huge rain would it be that deep anywhere near our fields. She'd lost her shoe in the muck and as she tried to free herself from the mud she lost her balance and landed on her rump in the glop. She was making lots of noises so I tried to move toward the sound, but there was a fence between us.

Together we sifted through the mud and tried to find her shoe. No way were we going back to the house without it. After digging around in the darkness she finally came up with her ill-fated mud-covered tennis shoe. Now when she walked she made a distinctive sound…a squishy, suck sound with every step. It sure made it easier to follow her with those sound effects.

It seemed we'd lost our bearings again so we searched the sky for our light…there it was behind us. We must've gotten turned around in the creek. Well we started back up the hill…with me stumbling along following the sounds of her sucking tennis shoe. Finally we reached the wooden fence along the lane…we climbed up the gate and jumped over into our barn lot. Suck, slop, plop…suck, slop, plop…suck, slop, plop…we didn't have far to go now… then suddenly her muddy shoe stopped making noise.

Right ahead of us was a huge, white, nice looking barn next to a pole light. There was no junk in this barn lot and there was all kinds of modern fancy tractors parked in a line next to the machine shed. This definitely was not our place.

Neither of us said a word. We both just stood there staring at the barn...wondering whose barn it was and how the heck we ended up here. There didn't seem to be a house anywhere around, just this really nice barn.

We both start talking at the same time...wondering where we were. We figured we'd crossed three...maybe four fences...neither of us remembered crossing any road...there was that deep creek and Mom even thought she might've tromped through someone's garden.

By that time I was cold and tired...I just wanted to stay there and sleep in the barn. Mom was determined to find her way home and give dad a piece of her mind...she was pretty sure he had something to do with our getting lost. Besides...the rule was...if anything went wrong, it was Dad's fault! And plenty had gone wrong that night.

Finally, we determined we were east of our place, so we headed back in the direction we figured had to be right...it wasn't long before mom's bloodhound skills kicked in and she found the tractor path that lead us home.

We found dad half-asleep in his chair with the TV blaring. His glasses had slid down his nose, and were tilted sideways...almost falling off his face. He had one shoe off and his other foot was resting on the coffee table.

When mom slammed the kitchen door, dad raised his head and started to mumble. Mom told him all about our adventure and said our pole light was out...it must've blown the bulb. Dad said it wasn't out...he had turned it off earlier.

That explanation made the hair stand straight up on my mother's head and she demanded to know "What in God's green earth" had made him turn off the pole light that night when never once...since we had moved to the place...could she get him to turn it off before!

Dad looked at her with an innocent expression...blinked his eyes a couple of times and said something about her wanting him to work at lowering the electric bill. He said she was always complaining about him leaving that light on all the time and he figured it was high time we started shutting it off when we came in for the evening...and that since he was in for the night...he turned it off.

Then there was some talk about the difference between *him* being in for the evening and *everybody* being in. That was followed by a reminder of the hike in the electric bill, and then final arguments were presented by both sides.

Before this discussion ended I'd plopped down on the sofa and drifted off to sleep. All that fresh air and exercise had done me in. I woke up in the middle of the night and heard mummers of conversation, interrupted by bursts of laughter. It was dark in the house and all the lights were off, so I got up from the couch and drug my tired body up the stairs to bed.

By the time morning came all was well again. The fog had lifted outside and seemed to have dissipated inside as well. Dad never had to worry 'bout mom givin' him the business for leaving the pole light on all the time...mom never had to worry about him turning it off if she was lost in the woods in the fog. As for me...well, I never had to worry much anyway...I always knew no matter what happened, mom and dad would get it all worked out okay.

CHAPTER
ELEVEN

DADDY'S
GIRL

B y the time I was nine my sister, Sharon, had moved on and was living in an apartment up by Chicago, Illinois. She had a job...her own place...her own furniture and no one told her what to wear or what to eat and she could do anything she pleased...and I was jealous.

After she'd had a couple of years to settle in, Sharon took to inviting me up for a visit each summer to stay with her for a week. I'd take the Greyhound bus to Chicago and then we'd ride the EL out to her place. For the next seven days we were friends instead of sisters...we'd go to the museums and the parks...ride the subway...she even showed me where she worked and introduced me to her friends.

Chicago was so much more exciting than our farm. People were different there, too...more elegant and refined. The parks had fountains with colored lights and there were zoos, plays and other interesting places to go. These visits were always enlightening and educational for me and even though I always wanted to go...I was always ready to return home when the time came, too.

The trip I'd like to tell you about was one of the trips home. I'd stayed an extra week that year so it was the end of June and I was gettin' homesick for my folks and my folks were homesick for me, too.

We'd enjoyed a good visit, but the extra week had taken its' toll. I'd gotten bored one day when she was at work so I tried to ride the subway alone and had gotten lost...which gave both of us a good scare. I was homesick and crabby, and she was ready to get rid of me for another year.

When we arrived at the bus station the woman at the counter said that the bus had some mechanical problem and was off schedule so we had to wait around for it to be replaced by a different bus…then I could be on my way.

Sharon said she'd call our folks when she got back to the apartment and let 'em know I was going to be late, then we settled in for the wait. Time seemed to drag…so when the new bus showed up I was ready to get on. But now…instead of getting home before dark…I wouldn't be home until after 10 o'clock. I'd be traveling through the night on a bus loaded with strangers.

Sharon thought that we maybe we should wait and try again in the morning but I had a really bad case of the blubbers from my homesickness, so she got some masking tape from the clerk and with a black marker wrote "Moline, Illinois" on the tape and stuck it to the front of my shirt. She said that way if I fell asleep someone would wake me up at my stop.

She handed me a sack with a bologna sandwich and an apple…told me not to talk to strangers and not to get off the bus 'til I saw mom and dad. Then she kissed my forehead…told me not to tell mom about the subway incident and I got on the bus. I found a seat by the window and waved at her as we pulled away. Then I started to cry again…I'm not sure what all the blubbering was about but I couldn't seem to help it…I cried until the hum of the engine put me to sleep.

When I woke up the bus was stopped and there were lots of people getting on and getting off. I asked where we were and if we were in Moline. The driver said we had a ways to go yet, so I went back to my seat. I didn't get off the bus, because Sharon had said to stay put until I saw mom 'n dad. She said they would be worried about me.

And they were…they'd left home for the bus station long before Sharon got back to her apartment to call them so they'd been waiting around for a long time. Finally they went inside to check with the clerk to see when my bus was suppose to arrive. Dad was pretty upset when he found out I'd be two hours late so he told everybody there how dangerous it was to have his little girl on a bus at night…and it was raining to boot! He told them how his baby girl had gone up to the big city, and how he'd worried the whole time I was gone. He said he didn't even like his older daughter livin' up there, but what could he do…she was all grown up. He went on to tell them stories about me and the things I'd done 'til Mom said she was so embarrassed she went out and got back in the truck. Mom said he kept talking 'bout me like I was still five years old.

Mom said there were two older ladies who really took up my dad's side and agreed it was too dangerous to have a little girl travel on a bus all the way from Chicago. Mom said they even walked outside and stood there in the parking lot while dad paced back and forth. She said every once in a while one of them would toss a nasty look her way…like she was a terrible mother for putting this little tiny girl in peril by placing her on a bus…alone…and sending her off to a big city. They kept wringing their hands and nodding their heads as dad talked.

Finally the woman with blue hair could stand it no longer…she walked over to our truck and gave my mom a piece of her mind! She told my momma how terrible she was for sending her little girl out into the cold cruel world alone. How she should be ashamed of herself. How no one in their right mind would put a small child on a bus from Chicago, of all places, and expect her to make it to the other side of Illinois in one piece. She told my momma they'd be lucky if anyone ever heard from me again! Then she went back to pacing and wringing her hands with my daddy.

Finally my bus pulled into the lot. Dad pert' near ran over all the people waiting in line to get to the door of the bus. Each time someone stepped out of the bus he'd ask if they'd seen his little girl. The two old women were standing right beside him, watching to be sure I was okay. They stood on their tip toes to peek in the bus and see if they could spot this small child traveling alone.

I was the last one off the bus. At fourteen I was five-feet seven-inches tall and I no longer gave the impression I was a "little girl" so neither of the women gave me a second glance as I passed them by. When I saw my father I yelled out "Here I am, Daddy!" Both of the women standing at the bus door turned around and stared at my dad and watched in amazement as he picked me up and swung me around in his arms.

The woman with the blue hair spoke first. "This is your *little* girl? My lands, I thought we were looking for a youngster…why this child is full grown!"

"This is my little girl!" Dad said happily.

"She's not so little." The second woman agreed.

"This is Doris...my little girl!" Daddy stated, still grinning from ear to ear.

"Mister, we thought you had a child on that bus!"

"Yep!" said my dad. "And here she is!"

Momma got out of the truck and I ran over and gave her a hug. The lady with the blue hair looked up at Mom and started to talk, but mom just raised her hand and shook her head and smiled.

Dad walked up behind us, threw my suitcase in the truck bed and I scrambled into my spot in the middle of the cab. He jumped in the driver's seat of the truck and gave the old ladies a grin and a wave and we were on our way.

Dad never had a clue that he'd mislead those two poor women. To him I was...and would always be...his baby girl. And to me...he was...and will always be my 'daddy'.

CHAPTER
TWELVE

the Big
War HERO

My dad always slept in his undershorts and t-shirt. He was a modest man, so we never really saw him at bed time, but we'd heard that's what he wore. Once…by accident, I found out for sure.

On the night I want to tell you about, Dad didn't go to work on second shift at the shop. He was off that night and we'd all turned in early. Well…sort of…Mom and Dad had turned in early and I had gone to my room, but I was sixteen and I had a boyfriend…and even though the rules at our house were no phone calls after nine o'clock…I was going to have my boyfriend call me at midnight. Did I mention I was sixteen…

Anyway…out our way all the phones were on a party line, which meant if the phone rang…you had to pick up the receiver…then press a little button on the side of the phone so you could take the call. The bonus attached this type of phone was, I'm sure, made just for me. Here's the scoop…if you held the receiver to your ear, you could hear the line buzz just before the phone would ring in the house. Now…if you had reflexes that allowed you to react at the speed of lighting you could punch the button and keep the phone from ringing…thereby getting a phone call in the middle of the night without your parents being any the wiser.

That was my plan. I waited quietly 'til I could hear the rhythm of my father's snores. Then I snuck down the steps, skipping the squeaky ones and pausing each time one made even the smallest sound. When I reached the bottom I crept through the living room…reached up and grabbed the phone's receiver. Then I laid down on the floor and waited for my Romeo to call. I had a long wait 'cause I was about a half hour early.

I kept one eye on the clock over by the stove in the kitchen, and tried to stay awake while I waited. When it was about three minutes before the love of my life was suppose to call...the fates turned on me.

There came a rustling from my parent's bedroom, dad stopped snoring and started coughing. The old bed squeaked and groaned, and the bedroom door creaked open. In the moonlight spilling into the kitchen I could see my dad entering the room and heading across the floor to the back porch...he must've been headed for the bathroom. I was crouched down in the doorway between the kitchen and the living room trying to blend in with the woodwork.

Dad took about two steps...realized he was not alone in the room and screamed for my mom. This man who was a World War II veteran was not prepared to do battle in his underwear. He let out a yelp and hollered "Jean! There's some man lying in the kitchen on the floor!" With that he turned on his heels and ran back in his bedroom and slammed the door.

Mom never got out of her warm bed. She just said "Doris, get up off that floor and hang up that phone, I know you are out there waiting for some boy to call you... now get up those stairs and go to bed".

I said what any girl caught in that situation would say. I said "I'm not waiting for anybody to call me I was just going to the bathroom."

83

Just then the phone rang...

I'd learned that when you find yourself in a bad situation, it's always best to tell the truth.

So I picked up the receiver...pushed the button...and said in my sweetest, most innocent voice, "I'm sorry, Romeo, but you know I can't take any phone calls after nine o'clock." then I hung up the receiver and went up to bed.

Just as I reached the top step, Mom reminded me about the bathroom.

I could never get away with anything. Whoever said 'You can fool some of the people some of the time' never met my mom 'cause you sure couldn't fool her...not even once.

When I came down for breakfast the next morning the clock had been moved so it was hanging right over the telephone and there was a note just below it that said I had no phone privileges for a week and that when I did get them back...I'd better make sure I knew what time it was before I answered the call. There was a 'P.S.' at the bottom of the page that read: "Don't be downstairs wandering around in the middle of the night anymore— it scares your dad."

CHAPTER
THIRTEEN

SMOKEY
THE
'n
CAR WASH

I was always trying to get a fella to pay attention to me when I was in junior high school. Usually it ended up I was attracting the wrong kinds of fellas or if I could get a nice guy to look at me…fate would prevail and I'd end up doing something so strange that I'd leave an impression…more often than not, the impression I left was not favorable so the fella I was trying to catch realized all to soon why he was staying away from me.

This was one of those days.

I'd started off the day on the wrong foot…I'd just wanted to run into town…check out the happenings and get back to the farm before my folks even knew I was missing. Now mind you…I was never suppose to ride Smokey into town and certainly never without a saddle. But on that day I was in a hurry so I took Smokey…bareback…right up Main Street…

There I was riding down the center of Main Street on that bright Saturday morning, checking out the sights. As I got up next to the newest addition in our little village…the car wash…much to my delight a really cute guy that I knew from school…who had just got his drivers license…was there with his car, rummaging through his pockets. It was obvious to me that this fine young man needed some help…and I could sure be a helpful kind of gal…so I rode Smokey right up next to him and inquired about his dilemma. Turned out all he needed was some change.

Change? I could get him some change! I could be a hero! All I had to do was run over to the "Royal Blue" and cash in a dollar and get four quarters. I made him an offer. I'd tie Smokey up there beside him and run to the store for change...all he had to do was keep an eye on my horse.

He surveyed the situation carefully...looked up at Smokey's head and said he didn't know anything about horses...ummm...he wasn't too sure.

I wanted to be helpful in the worst way so I told him Smokey was okay...pretty gentle as a matter of fact. I told him Smokey looked a little scary but he wouldn't do anything 'cept stand there 'til I got back. The guy was still a little hesitant, so I assured him that all the rumors he'd heard about Smokey were just that...rumors. I told him he had nothing to fear but fear itself...Smokey wasn't nearly as wild as people thought or I wouldn't be able to ride him bareback! However, I neglected to tell him Smokey was terrified of water...whenever he saw a water hose he had a tendency to rear and bite...I really didn't see any reason to bring all that up, after all...there were no hoses lying around anyway.

Even though the object of my attention didn't seem to want my help...I dismounted...tied Smokey's reins to the downspout of the car wash building and headed for the grocery store across the street.

I ran in...grabbed the change and started out the door. Smokey hadn't been outta my sight for an entire minute, 'cause I could see everything through the big windows in the front of the store.

Well...just as I started back across the street the fella chucked a quarter into the car wash...apparently he'd found one in his car. The kid stood there with the sprayer in his hand and Smokey was eyeing him with suspicion and already trying to back up…that's when the water shot out of the sprayer… and well…

Smoke started rearing and whinnying, running and jumping…that scared the kid so much that he threw the sprayer down. When the hose landed it spun around on the floor of the car wash and spayed water right into Smokey's face.

Uh, oh…I started running for my horse…I knew that Smokey and water didn't mix. About that time Smokey reared and caused the downspout to break loose from the building. It made a big banging sound when it hit the ground. Unfortunately, I'd tied Smokey's reins tight to the pipe so he couldn't get himself free. He kicked his hind feet a few times…shook his head with his mouth open, which made the kid run out of the car wash screaming, and then with one final jump and rear Smoke managed to pull all of the downspout and most of the drain pipe clear off the building. Then he was loose, well…kinda…he was still attached to the downspout by his reins…and the downspout was still connected to the drainpipe…the entire calamity was too much for Smokey.

He started running for home…right down Main Street. The pipes from the car wash kept banging on the road as he ran. Every once in a while he'd stop for a second and kick at them…then take off at warp speed again. He was more than a little confused…his eyes were wide as saucers and he was snorting and whinnying. It created a kind of a bang-bang-snort-whinny-rear-kick sequence…and it was

LOUD. I was sure that people a hundred miles a way were wondering what the racket was about.

At first I tried to run after him...I thought maybe I could catch him and fix everything up. But a block into the chase I realized he was way faster than I knew. Besides people were coming out of the little café and the gas station to see what all the commotion was about. All I could do was hope that no one would know it was my horse, so I turned off on the next block figuring that I might be able to intercept him at the edge of town.

No such luck...by the time I got over to the last block I could see Smokey rounding the bend a good quarter mile ahead of me, and he was picking up speed. I looked back down the road the other way...bits and pieces of the drainage system of the car wash littered the blacktop...my heart was pounding and thoughts of runnin' away from home were racing through my head. Finally, I decided I'd better just get home and face the music.

I ran as far as I could before I had to stop and catch my breath. Smokey was clean out of sight, but I could see the trail he left...it was marked with pieces of metal that littered the road leading to my house. There were too many pieces for me to pick up and carry so I decided to just toss them in the ditch as I went.

When I got to the hill before our house the longest piece of the downspout was laying in the road so I picked it up and carried it the rest of the way home. By the time I got to the front yard, someone had tied Smokey to the tree next to the house, and there was a bucket of water in front of him. He was soaked wet with sweat and still stomping his feet.

The last piece of the downspout was laying on the back porch…I knew this day wasn't going very well…but what else could possibly go wrong?

As I came through the kitchen door my heart sank…there on the phone was DAD! It was obvious he was talking to the owner of the car wash. "Yep, that's my horse…" Yep…it was his kid, too! Yep…yep… and finally he said "Okay, Bart, I'll be up later and we'll take care of it. Okay, then, Goodbye"

Mom was standing over by the kitchen sink with her arms crossed watching my dad and when I came in and sat down she gave me one of her "looks"…the one that meant I was going to be working all summer to make up for this one day when I had a lapse in good judgment.

When dad hung up the phone he turned and looked at me…pushed his little blue cap back on his head and plopped down on his chair at the table. His glance moved from me to mom…I think he was having trouble deciding where to start. I knew I'd better just spill my guts…there was too much evidence stacked against me.

So I told my folks how I had only been going to be in town a few minutes…how Smokey never left my sight…how I didn't know a horse could pull that hard…how that kid should've just waited for me to get back before he started the car wash…I told them what *should've* have happened but *didn't*. Then they told me what *should'nt* have happened but *did*…and what WAS going to happen next.

And life went back to normal…the owner of the car wash turned out to be an okay guy…he and my dad got the drainage system back together. Smokey survived…although he never did learn to like water. Mom's facial expressions went back to normal by the next morning…and as for me…well a little hard work over the summer didn't hurt me either.

I learned at least a couple of lessons from that day…whenever I rode Smokey bareback into town I never tied him to a downspout. But mostly I learned that being able to see your horse is not the same as being able to CONTROL your horse. Later on in my life I found that's true out about other things too…my hair, for instance or my kids, especially my kids…but that's a whole other set of stories!

CHAPTER
FOURTEEN

THE HUNTER 'n THE FIREWORKS

One of the problems we had out at the farm were the hunters...guys who'd sneak over the fence in the woods and bring their flashlights and dogs with them. It did no good to call anyone in authority for help, by the time they arrived to hand out any fine the guys would be long gone. I guess even if you have a woods full of livestock it is also full of deer and other woodland creatures and that just makes it too tempting to the hunters, so we had to come up with our own way of making them behave.

Over the years we had devised our special plan of action. We found out that if we got between the hunters and their hounds and set off a string of firecrackers, the sound would frighten the dogs into running away. The hunters then had to spend the rest of the night looking for their precious dogs and we didn't have to worry so much about any of our animals being mistaken for a deer and getting shot. This plan seemed to work best for us, so we had an entire drawer in the kitchen dedicated to the firecrackers needed to fend off any hunters.

We had a huge selection of strings, in every color and size. At the first sound of the hounds, we'd pick up our weapon of choice and head down to the woods. Once we found our spot, we'd light the whole rack and throw them on the ground in the lane to scare off the dogs. Then we'd run back up to the house, snickering under our breath.

It was never very long after we 'd carried out our attack that we'd start to hear the whistling and name calling that often went on for hours while the hunters searched for their dogs. Far in the distance you might hear a dog bark his response. Eventually the hunters figured out what we were doing so our woods saw fewer and fewer repeat customers...they all knew we had a drawer full of firecrackers and we were not afraid to use them.

On one particular night a fog was rollin' in and we'd been hearing the hunter's dogs for about an hour. Dad decided this was a die-hard hunter, and we best get rid of him. I offered to walk down the lane and do the job...I'd done it lots of times before and I knew the routine.

So I set off with a big strip of 'crackers in my pocket...I crossed through the orchard and down over the first hill 'til I was close to one of the dogs. I could hear him plain so I figured he must be right over the ridge...I looked for the clearing and decided to set off my bounty. I moved out into the lane where the fog was so thick I could barely see my hand in front of my face.

I bent down and felt for the road...lit a match and set off the string of firecrackers. Oops...I'd misjudged my location so now I had to throw them in the air to get rid of them. I gave them a fling down the lane and they started popping off.

That was when I realized the hunter was standing right where I threw my load. He let out a yelp and a few swear words then his flashlight flew up in the air. I heard his footsteps as he started running down the lane in one direction...his dogs were bellowing and running the other way. Uh, oh...the hunter was headed right for me so I turned around and started running for the house, but he was more scared than I was...he caught up to me and ran right past me there in the darkness. I heard another swear word or two as he went over the hill.

I slowed down my pace and started trotting up to the house. The operation had not gone exactly as I'd hoped, but it seemed the hunter was on his way home and that was the overall plan anyway.

Well the next evening a big, fancy, red pick-up truck pulled up in our driveway. We all came out to see who the city slicker was…a little, short, stocky fellow climbed down out of the cab and told us he'd lost two of his dogs in the fog the night before and he thought they might have run off in our woods. He said he wanted to be sure we knew he was just looking for his dogs so that no one would shoot at him if he went on into the woods and looked around.

He said he'd been over at the neighbors the night before and some maniac had set off a bunch of fireworks and scared his dogs off and that he had to leave before he could find them. He said only idiots used firecrackers to scare other people's dogs and that some people didn't use the common sense they were born with. He went on with his little tirade and said lots of unkind things and alluded to the fact that we weren't much better than all the other hillbilly's he'd had to deal with in the past. The little man looked me over good…like he was trying to decide if I was the one he'd passed on the lane.

I stood up straight and looked him right in the eye. Maniac, huh? Hillbilly, huh? We'd see about that!

Dad said it was okay for him to go look for his dogs 'cause we didn't want them down there chasing our sheep.

I waited for him to reach the orchard then headed into the house...I'd never had much patience for people who stooped low enough to call me names! I opened the 'cracker drawer and picked out a dozen of the biggest, longest rows I could find. Then I took off the back way into the woods...crossed over through the bean field...found my spot in the walnut grove near the clearing next to the road...and took my position. I was pretty sure it wouldn't be much of a wait before the hunter found his way to the clearing. It was getting dark out in the woods and I could see the beam from his flashlight as he walked along the valley. I started tying the stands together until I had a big half circle right there in the middle of the clearing. Then I hid behind a log...

Here came Mr. High 'n Mighty, with his two dogs on leashes. This was going to be fun...

Just as he entered the clearing I reached out from behind the log and set off my circle. The dogs started to run in every direction. Well the little man still had ahold of the leashes so when the dogs ran back and forth he got all tangled up as the leashes wrapped around his legs. He let out a holler as he landed on his butt on the hard ground. Now the dogs were trying to run in different directions but they were too tangled up with their master so they just drug him back and forth through the brambles.

I was laughing pretty hard when I stood up from behind the log...gave him a wave and headed back to the house. "Sticks 'n stones will break your bones".... But words can do more damage...I hope he got the message.

CHAPTER
FIFTEEN

BEE 'n DAD

M y dad was a tall skinny guy with big hands 'n big ears. I don't know if his ears were really that big, or if they just looked big because he kept his hair short. Maybe it was that little blue cap that made them look so gigantic.

For the most part dad was a pretty easy going guy and could get along with almost anybody, and any animal, too. Except for bees...dad 'n bees just didn't get along....ever. Bee's really liked to sting him...they stung him often and he didn't like it much when they did.

Mom on the other hand, never had much trouble with bees. In fact, they would land on her once in a while but hardly ever stung her. She said it was because she tasted bad but I think it was because even the insects knew better than to tick her off.

Anyway, the day I want to tell you about we'd been putting up hay in the barn when dad ran into trouble...he'd uncovered a nest of bees. They chased him around for awhile before he decided to get some backup...he went up to the house to get mom and told her she had to get rid of the nest of bees so he could get back to work.

She preformed her usual ritual...she dug around in the hay and found the center of the nest. Then as soon as she got the bees all stirred up she'd spray 'em with some concoction she'd mixed up. It never took very long for the bees to decide that all they could do was leave their happy home and look for a new place to build their nest.

Well on this day Dad was keeping his distance so the bees wouldn't find him and as she was finishing up her eviction notice so we could get on with the work at hand, all of us kids sat on the rack wagon and marveled at the fact that she never got stung...no matter how mad she made the bees.

After the bees were gone we finished putting up the hay and it was looking like things were all going to work out...

The last load was in for the afternoon and everyone 'cept my daddy had gone on into the house to clean up. We'd stripped off our jeans and long sleeved shirts...had a shower and were all sitting out on the picnic table drinking some lemonade...enjoying the rewards of a job well done. It was peaceful and quiet and cool there in the shade of the old elm trees.

Dad was still out in the barn lot putting away the tractor and the wagon and probably just messing 'round wasting time 'til dinner. He was over by the machine shed...at least that is where he was when the ruckus started.

From up at the house it sounded like he was in the midst of a fight...there was lots of swearing 'n yelling...it sounded like he was throwing things...then suddenly the ruckus died down and dad came out of the barn lot looking pretty beat up.

He was walking with a limp...kinda dragging one leg and he had one hand on his back and the other one covering one ear...His shirt was pert' near torn off and his jeans were on kinda sideways and he was muttering to himself as he walked...saying things I don't think I should repeat.

When he got up to the yard we all ran over to see if we could help him. He looked pretty upset and as if he was in bad shape. Mark picked up a big stick and gave it to Dad so he could walk easier.

Mom beat me over to him and asked "what in God's green earth" had happened!

Daddy said something nasty about the bees…seemed they'd got after him when he was putting the tractor in the shed. He'd tried to jump off the seat but his shirt got caught, so he'd grabbed his shirt and tore it so he could get away, but all the bees kept chasing him. He'd taken off running…around the side of an old box car we used as a barn for the sheep…when he'd rounded the corner he'd slipped in some sheep manure…fallen flat on his back…hurt his leg and 'bout broke his back all the while the dang bees just kept stinging him on his big old ear. I wished you could've heard him tell it…

Mom said she'd better get something for his ear…she barely made it to the kitchen door before she burst out laughing. She had been trying to hold it in so's not to hurt his feelings. I'd followed her in and I started laughing too. Then the rest of the bunch came in and we busted up…the laughter was spreading like a wild fire. Most of us were laughing so hard we couldn't even speak.

Dad was sittin' outside on one of the lawn chairs hollering "I can hear all of you in there laughin' at me!"…the more he yelled…the more we laughed! "You wouldn't be laughin' if them bees were after your hide!" He bellowed…wasn't too long though, before he started laughin' too.

It took a while but I finally got my breath back and my laughin' fit was almost under control, so mom handed me a vat of salve for his ear...an ice pack for his leg and a fresh glass of lemonade. I headed outside to get my dad fixed up.

You'd think the worst was over...but no...we'd spilled lemonade on the picnic table earlier and it wasn't long before the bees came a callin' again.

Dad was still sitting in his chair and we were still all laughing when he spied one of the bees...he let out a yelp and jumped up out of the chair...knocking it over in the yard! He threw the ice pack at the bee, swung his walking stick about like crazy and finally flung his lemonade at the lone bee. Suddenly there bees everywhere...buzzing all about and dive bombing him from every direction! Dad was doing some kind of weird dance as he tried escape the attack and when he bolted toward the kitchen door he lost his footing and fell smack to the ground...that's when the bees swooped in and stung him a bunch of times on his other ear...

Now both of his ears were swollen and if we thought they were big before...well now we're talking major sized monster ears! They were standing straight out from his head...red as fire with bumps and lumps all over 'em. To top it off we lathered him up with so much salve that they had white rims around the edges and well...let's just say, they definitely caught your attention.

As luck would have it about an hour after the bee incident was over, a fella stopped by to find out about having some hay delivered for his horses. This guy'd heard we had some hay to sell, so when he came asking about it, we let him into the kitchen where dad was sitting at the table.

The man was trying to find out how much hay we had available and how much it would cost to have a couple of loads delivered, but he had some trouble getting his words out. He'd never met dad before, so I guess he wasn't sure if dad just had enormous ears or if there'd been an accident. He kept staring at my dad's ears and each time he'd open his mouth to speak he'd get about three words out then stop in mid-sentence and just stare.

Dad didn't seem to notice…guess he just figured this guy wasn't much of a talker…so dad asked the questions 'bout how much hay and where to deliver it and all the while the fella just stood there with his mouth open and nodding. Even though dad had all the information he needed to get the job done the guy kept standing there…waiting. Well 'cause dad loved to talk to anybody who'd listen…and this guy seemed like a nice enough fella…dad got him a cup of coffee…pulled a chair over for his new audience and told him three or four of his funny stories…but never once, did he mention the bees or his ears. The man just sat there staring at dad and nodding as the stories went on and on…

Finally the visitor couldn't stand it any longer…so he asked my dad if he knew he had white stuff on his ears. Yup…Daddy said, he knew it…but still he didn't offer him any explanations…

After a long while, daddy stood up and told the fella he had chores to get done…the man nodded and as Daddy walked toward the guy and he got up out of his chair and started backing out of the kitchen door. Well dad backed him up all the way down the sidewalk 'til he got to his truck...then dad opened the door and helped him in...the whole time this guy just kept nodding and staring at my dad's humongous ears.

We stood there in the front yard and watched as the truck disappear over the first hill...wondering what the heck dad was going to do next.

Dad just shook his head and glanced down at the ground. "Poor thing" he said. "I bet people tease him 'cause he stutters like that...don't you kids be laughing at him... 'cause I know I'd hate it if there was some reason people poked fun at me..."

And with that he turned and headed back to the barnyard to finish his day.

CHAPTER
SIXTEEN

O'
Christmas
Tree

Thanksgiving dishes were done and Christmas was coming! Time to get the house in order and decorated for the holiday season!

The year before someone had given us one of those aluminum trees...the ones that looked like they were made out of curly tin foil...it had a little colored disk that sat at the bottom and reflected color onto the shiny branches. I don't know if you ever had one, but my mom hated ours. It was one of those things that looked better in the store than it did once we got it in our living room.

That year at Thanksgiving dinner Mom announced she was going to have a real tree and she refused to put up the tinfoil tree ever again. She said she didn't care if needles got in the carpet, it would still be better than that fake silver tree. Then she took the tinfoil tree out and put it in the trash barrel so there would be no mistaking the fact that we were getting a real tree for Christmas.

Now my dad believed that buying a tree that'd been cut down was a waste of money. He felt the same way about cut flowers...he'd say that once they were cut, they were dead and who'd be dumb enough to spend their hard earned money on dead flowers and trees? But with it being Christmas and all, he wanted to make my mom happy, so he promised he'd get her a real tree.

The days came and went...then a full week went by and Mom was getting a little miffed that we didn't have our tree up and decorated. She mentioned it to dad now and again before she finally decided to take matters into her own hands...

One evening while Dad was away at work and the snow was just beginning to fall...she told me to get my coveralls on...we were going to get us a Christmas tree. After I'd gotten myself all dressed for the weather, she produced a hand saw and a toboggan and down in the woods we went.

Now we didn't have any of those pretty, regular pine trees out our way, but we did have a bunch of white pines we'd planted the first year we moved there. We'd gotten about two hundred little seedlings and planted them all over the place. Most of them had died, but fifty or so had taken root and hung on...apparently mom and I were going to cut one of those down for our Christmas tree.

There we were...out in our woods...trying to picture what each tree would look like all decorated up in our front window. We finally decided on what seemed to be the perfect tree and after much grunting and groaning...huffing and puffing...sawing and dragging we finally got the tree up to the house. Let me tell you...dragging a tree out of the woods...in the snow...on a make shift toboggan was no easy task.

We managed to drag the tree up to the door and that's when we found out that trees sure look a lot smaller when they're in the woods then they do when they're in your house...this one was about three feet too tall, so we cut off some branches. We still had trouble gettin' it into the house, and we even broke the window in the storm door in the process.

After we got it into the living room and into the tree stand we couldn't get it to stand up straight...the trunk was bent in the middle...so we got it as straight as we could then we lopped off the top to keep it from looking like it was leaning over. With the top cut out it looked a little like a leaning volcano. It took hours of hard labor before we finally got it to stand up.

We decorated it with all our new ornaments and used tinsel to fill in the big gaps between the branches...white pines have about 12 inches between the branches so there were lots of pretty big gaps and we used lots of tinsel.

The tree still looked bare...

We dug boxes of old ornaments out of the attic...we strung popcorn and cranberries...we even made more ornaments out of styrofoam balls and pinecones.

It still looked bare...

Mom took some of the packages she'd already wrapped and instead of placing the gifts under the tree we strategically placed them between the branches.

It still needed something...

So, mom dug out some red and green construction paper and we made paper chains to hang on each of the branches. We also made picture frames out of old cardboard we'd painted and hung pictures of everyone in our family from the ten branches of our enormous tree.

It still looked pretty sad...

Finally, mom said it was getting late and I should go up to bed. I knew she was upset with our meager yet heroic attempt to have a real Christmas tree, so I told her that I thought it looked wonderful! I wanted to make her feel better. She gave me a hug and told me not to worry...it would all work out...so I went upstairs...climbed under my quilt and fell asleep.

Throughout the night I thought I heard the roar of power tools from time to time, but I was so tired that after a minute or two the noise would stop and I would drift off to sleep again.

The next morning when I came down the stairs I saw what all the racket had been about during the night. Mom had retrieved the tin foil tree from the trash heap...drilled holes in the tree trunk of the white pine and stuck the silver branches of the tin foil tree in the holes to fill in the gaps between the branches of the real tree. It was...an interesting solution....not exactly one of her better ideas, but at least the tree didn't look so bare. As mom stood there grinning at me I wasn't quite sure what to say. She put her arm around my shoulder and said for me not to worry...it was all going to work out. I just nodded and smiled...got dressed and headed off to school.

That afternoon when I got off the school bus, I was surprised to see our truck waiting at the end of our lane. Mom and Dad were both inside, and I knew something big was going on in order for him not to be at work. As soon as I climbed in the cab they announced we were going into town to buy us a Christmas tree.

As we walked up and down the aisles inspecting each tree, Dad said we could have which ever one we pleased, money was no object! He said he'd do almost anything to get that "monstrosity" out of our living room. We marched right up to the front of the tree lot where the expensive trees were standing with the blue tapes on the branches. We picked a nice tall, full tree with long fragrant needles. A man in a stocking cap said we'd made an excellent choice and he loaded our beautiful tree into the back of the truck.

I guess mom's solution wasn't so bad after all. She kept telling me not to worry...it would all work out. Guess she knew that if our beat up tree looked bad enough then dad would have to take action and she was right.

When it was all said and done, it turned out to be a great day. Dad helped us decorate the tree and the house...the three of us sang every Christmas carol we knew while we worked...we all drank hot chocolate together and had plenty of popcorn strung to hang out for the birds. That year we had the most beautiful tree I've ever seen...but then...I've never to this day seen one quite as ugly as the first tree, either.

It's good to remember that even when things look pretty bleak...you should never give up hope...it will all work out in the end. And sometimes if things are bad enough it's alright to toss out the old and start fresh.

CHAPTER

SEVENTEEN

GLAMOUR
GIRL

When I was growing up I used to read magazines made specially for teenage girls. I'd look at all the pretty pictures of the models and want to be like them. I didn't know they doctored up the pictures so the girls looked better than they did in real life, I just thought they'd found a pool of beautiful teenagers who never had acne. I was jealous and determined to look as beautiful as they did.

The summer I was sixteen I worked extra hard at it and you could tell by looking at me...I'd made some significant changes...I didn't necessarily look better...just different.

I am willing to admit at least a couple of things I tried.

First was the cellar door incident...

I'd seen in that magazine how all the models had those beautiful streaks of blonde mingled with their dark hair. Well, you could buy this stuff that you sprayed in your hair where ever you wanted to be blonde, then you'd go out in the sun and let nature take its course. By the end of the day you were suppose to have the most fabulous blonde highlights and you'd look beautiful...I figured it had to be true 'cause the magazine said so.

Soon as I got my next paycheck from the ice cream parlor, I headed for the store and bought a couple of bottles of the highlighting spray. The next morning I was up with the chickens...ready to make my hair gorgeous. I read the directions thoroughly...looked in the mirror to determine where I wanted my blonde to be...and after careful consideration I decided that I wanted more than just highlights...I wanted to be a *beautiful blonde babe*.

It made sense to me that if a little bit of that spray made blonde streaks, then...surely if I just washed my hair with the solution...well, I would be a blonde bombshell by lunchtime!

Mom and Dad had gone into town and I had taken the morning off from work so I could concentrate on my beautification plan.

I took my bag of goodies into the bathroom...stuck my head in the sink and poured two bottles of the solution onto my long, thick, very dark brown hair. Then I put on my bathing suit...squirted myself with some baby oil so my dark, dirty-looking farmer's tan would turn a beautiful golden color...went out and laid down on the cellar door on the south side of our house to begin my transformation.

Two or three times in the first ten minutes I went in to check myself out in the mirror but I couldn't see any difference, so I went back to my spot on the cellar door. I had confidence in my plan and was sure that by the time my folks got home they'd have trouble recognizing me with my golden tan and my blonde hair! I was so excited!

Well I guess I must've fallen asleep as I basked in the warm sun 'cause the next thing I knew Mom was standing over me...kicking the bottom of my feet and telling me to go wash that stuff out of my hair and get some clothes on.

I jumped up and ran into the bathroom so I could see my new blonde locks in the mirror. OH NO...my hair wasn't blonde...it was a funny orangish color...no streaks of blonde...just orange. I quickly jumped into the shower and proceeded to shampoo my hair...five times I washed and rinsed it but it still was orange. My thick, long, dark brown hair looked like stringy, uneven, orange straw...it stood straight out from my head and made a crackly sound when I brushed it.

Not good...it didn't even feel like hair when I touched it...it was more like a corn broom that had gotten syrup stuck in between the straws. I called my mom to come and help me.

Mom washed it a couple more times then decided that we better call my oldest sister, Becky, for help. She came out that night and did her best to correct the problem. She cut my hair then she dyed it brown...she cut some more...then some more...by the end of the night there wasn't much left of my formerly thick, long, dark brown hair. Now it barely covered my ears...I had bangs again and yes it was brown, but not the brown color I had before.

Now not only was my hair straight...it was stiff as a board and it took two cans of hairspray to keep it from jutting out in funny angles. Finally, Becky decided that there wasn't much more she could do...she said that it would eventually grow out and she hoped I'd learned my lesson and that from now on I better not put anything in my hair except shampoo.

Well, I sort of learned my lesson at least regarding hair...I moved on from wanting to have blonde hair to trying to have shapely eyebrows. The girls in the magazines had eyebrows thinned into a perfect shape and both of them matched...it was exactly the way I wanted to look. My eyebrows were thick and heavy and sort of looked like one big black willy-worm stuck on my forehead. So into town I went. I bought tons of eye makeup in every color combination the magazine suggested for brunettes with hazel eyes…and I bought a good pair of tweezers. Then I returned home and studied the examples in the magazine. There were detailed instructions on how to shape your eyebrows by holding a pencil from the end of your nose to the outside of your eye and then plucking… yup, plucking is what they called it.

"Plucking" sounded easy to me…I could pluck…

I opened the little mirror I had on my dresser…drew a line over my eyebrow just like they said…then I grabbed one of my eyebrow hairs and gave it a yank…

Yeow…that HURT! Whew…my eyes started watering and my nose was running. Wow…I had to be doing it wrong! I read the article again. No…that was definitely what they said to do. Must be that one hair was just hooked in there deep…I'd decided to try again. I leaned over the mirror and gave another hair a yank…whew-whee…that stung! I sneezed a few times, wiped my eyes and sniffed. Who thought of this idea? Were they nuts? I knew I'd never make it through both eyebrows, actually I knew right then and there I couldn't even get one brow done at this rate…I still had about a thousand hairs to go. There had to be an easier way than this, besides the girl in the article was smiling! It shouldn't have that hurt *that* much!

I took my magazine article and my new makeup and started down the steps. I went into the bathroom, turned on both lights and locked the door.

I washed my face in hot water thinking that might loosen up the old eyebrow hairs. I took my tweezers...climbed up on the counter...leaned into the mirror and grabbed a couple of hairs at once. That way I would get done twice as fast! I gave 'em a good yank...let out a yelp and fell off the counter. Okay...no more of that for me! Enough was enough...there had to be a better way!

I threw my tweezers in the waste basket...opened the drawer beside the sink and began to search for some other tool to do the job. After an exhaustive search I found one...dad's razor! I could just shave off the hairs I didn't want. That could work...that would be easy!

I took out my new eyebrow pencil again and drew a line around the hairs I wanted to keep. Everything else I was going to trim off. I started on the left and shaved a few hairs off...ummm...not too bad. I moved to the right and tried to do the same pattern. Oops...I'd taken a little more off on the right, so I went back to make the left eyebrow match. One things for sure...trimming eyebrows with a double edged razor is not an easy job! Oh shoot...now I'd taken too much off the left one and had to make the one on the right a little more narrow. Crud...back to the left...gee...they're really getting thin...okay, just one more trim... that should do it. Oh crap! I have NO eyebrows at all! All that's left are two bright white streaks above my eyes that gave my face this stunned look of disbelief. Great...now what am I going to do?

I couldn't go out in public looking like this...what to do...what to do. I dug out my eyebrow pencil and tried to draw on eyebrows…that didn't work…I looked like a cartoon character. One was up high, the other down low…one was thicker than the other…not good…so I washed that off which left me with red steaks where the white ones had been. I was running out of options…panic was setting in. I jerked open the vanity drawer again, there just had to be something in there that would save me. I rummage through all the stuff that had been tossed into that junk drawer until BINGO, I found the answer. There in the bottom were the little tiny bandaid strips that had come in a box along with the big ones. No one at our house ever had a cut that small, so they'd been cast aside and made their way to the bottom of the junk drawer.

I pulled them out and held them up to the red steaks above my eyes…they were almost the perfect size. I placed one over each streak at a 45 degree angle…gathered up the makeup and the rest of the surplus bandaids then left the bathroom as if nothing unusual had happened.

I walked through the kitchen past my mother and sister-in-law who were chatting about the day's events. As I wandered by, the conversation ceased and they watched me as I made my way to the stairs. 'What in tarnation are you doin' with those bandaids plastered to your face?' mom demanded. I decided to show her…and for once she had nothing to say.

She knew I was feeling pretty bad about the whole deal, so she tried to be sympathetic. She helped me draw on my eyebrows for the next couple of weeks until mine grew back, and it wasn't long before I started looking like myself again.

I learned a couple of important lessons that summer...I learned that no matter how hard I tried I was probably never going to be one of the beautiful blonde models on the front page of a magazine and I learned that if plucking eyebrows was what it took to be a model...then I didn't want to be in a magazine that bad anyway. But mostly I learned that it is okay to just be me...to do the best I can with what I have and to be content with the end results.

CHAPTER
EIGHTEEN

DRIVEN'
'em CRAZY

L earning to drive should've come easily to me, after all I knew how to drive the tractors and had driven them all over the farm, how much harder could it be to drive the truck?

I was so anxious to get my drivers license that I was about to split. My birthday didn't come around 'til August which made me one of the youngest kids in my grade. That meant I wouldn't even have my learning permit until school was out for the summer. I was going to be about the last one in my class to climb behind the steering wheel of the school's drivers education car. Everyone I knew had their license except me…it was going to be a long summer.

As soon as I got my piece of paper that said I could drive a car as long as an adult was with me, I started to beg to drive. In fact anytime I saw an adult I asked if they'd let me drive their car so I could practice. Unfortunately I didn't get any takers, and my mom and dad told me to stop cornering everybody who stopped by the farm. Mom said that as soon as we got home from vacation she'd take me out and teach me to drive the red truck.

Mom was good about keeping her word, so I knew that once she'd made the promise it would happen…it wouldn't be long before I'd be behind the wheel of the old Ford.

Sure enough the day finally came…

Mom was going to do the laundry in town…so I loaded the last basket into the back of the truck then I opened the passenger side of the cab, climbed in and slammed the door. Mom walked around the truck…opened my door and asked me what I was doin' in her seat. With that she handed me the keys and told me this was the day she was going to teach me to drive.

Well I was grinnin' from ear to ear as I slid behind the big old steering wheel…I stuck the keys in the ignition and put my foot on the clutch pedal. I shoved the clutch all the way to the floor and fiddled with the gear shift until I got it in reverse. Then I let out on the clutch…the truck died. In fact, for the next fifteen minutes, every time I let out on the clutch…the truck died. I figured there had to be something wrong with the truck.

My confidence was starting to fade…

Finally, mom said she'd back the pickup out into our lane then let me take over. She guessed that it was probably the backing up part that was not working and wagered that I'd be able to drive it forward. So I climbed out of the cab and watched with my hands on my hips…sure she was going to find out there was something wrong with the engine. I stood there waiting for the motor to die as soon as she started to back up…hmmmm…no problem…she backed 'er right into our lane, lickety split.

Well, at least now the truck was running right, so I slid behind the wheel again…pushed my hair out of my face…licked my lips and gritted my teeth as I put it into first gear. When I took my foot off the brake so I could put it on the gas pedal, the truck started to slowly roll forward. Whoa… I wasn't ready to roll yet! I quickly slammed my foot back on the brake. Mom told me to give it some gas…I tried to explain how I couldn't give it any gas 'cause as soon as I took my foot off the brake the truck started to roll and it wasn't suppose to roll until I gave it permission.

She said I had to let off the clutch to keep it from rolling. Oh…that made sense…I popped the clutch…the truck died. Mom scratched her head…took a deep breath and explained that I had to push on the gas pedal at the same time I let off the clutch. Then she leaned forward and braced herself with the dashboard as she added in a rather matter of fact way that I had to give it some gas to make it go.

I started the engine again…

I let off the clutch and pushed on the accelerator…the truck died but kept rolling.…I slammed on the brakes.

I repeated this sequence about thirty times until we had made it to the bottom of the little hill in front of the house.

At that time mom took her hands and rubbed them up and down on her face. She gritted her teeth and picked her words carefully…trying not to sound upset. She said ALL I NEEDED TO DO WAS LET OFF THE CLUTCH…AT THE SAME TIME…I PUSHED ON THE GAS PEDAL. She said we needed to get into town to get the laundry done and at the rate we were going we would still be in our lane next week.

Okay, I got it. Now that we're at the bottom of the hill, maybe the truck wouldn't roll…if that was the case then I was sure I could do it. I took my foot off the brake…gave the old accelerator the heave ho…let off the clutch and the truck jump forward. It bucked a little but we were moving…finally.

I didn't get far before you could hear the engine whining for me to switch gears. Mom said to push in on the clutch and shift to second. I put the clutch in and slammed on the brake...oops...not right...the truck died. This time I only killed the engine three or four times and we were on our way again. Before long we'd made it to the end of our lane. I was starting to break a sweat, my mouth was dry and I was in awe of how hard it was to drive the truck.

Once or twice mom asked me if I wanted to keep going or if I'd learned enough for the day but I begged her to give me another chance 'cause I hadn't even been out on the open road yet.

Finally she agreed...

Well I stayed at the corner of our lane...looking up and down the road 'til the time came when there was not another car in sight. Then I shoved that accelerator pedal down hard so the engine was really racing and I let off the clutch. The truck jumped forward...let out a heave and I let off the gas a little. We bucked and jumped for a while and then...well then...I was driving on the hard road!

Mom was saying to give it a little more gas, so I did...just enough to keep it running. We were only going about 20 mph but I felt like we were moving at the speed of sound. I didn't want to go any faster 'cause then I'd have to shift and that hadn't gone so well the time before. Mom was saying to give it some more gas when I looked in the rear view mirror and saw a car behind us. Oh, Lord...what now?

Finally I gave it more gas at Mom's prodding...then shifted into second. That took awhile 'cause first I had to find second…then I had to let off the clutch. By then I had slowed down so much that second was too high of a gear so the truck started gasping and choking. Finally it died and the car behind me went around us…that was good.

This time I started it back up…got to a high enough speed to switch gears…found second and before I knew it we were sailing along at about 30 miles an hour…the wind was blowing through my hair. This was good…this was a speed I could handle. I crept up on the accelerator and it wasn't long before the truck was begging to be shifted into third gear so I took a deep breath…pushed in on the clutch and moved the gear shift once more. Third gear!

Now I was sailing along the blacktop at almost forty! Whew-hew…I'd done it…I'm was actually driving! Uh-oh, I could see a curve coming up ahead, so I began to slow down. No sense going around a bend at that kind of break neck speed. I was getting a little closer to the curve and could see that there was a car coming the other way and it was scheduled to pass me while I was in 'the curve'. I was terrified…I licked my lips and slowed down even more. My white knuckles were clinched around the steering wheel…the truck engine was making a sputtering sound and mom was telling me to give it more gas.

All I could think was that she'd gone insane…surely she could see that maniac driving right toward me! Oh well, she must know, so I gave it a little more gas and mom let out a sigh. We made it around the curve and I took it back up to 35 mph. Thirty-five was a good speed out there on the open highway. Thirty-five was just right. Then Mom said that even grandma drove faster than I did and that she wanted to get to the laundromat by nightfall. She told me to goose it and get up some speed or pull over and let her drive. She looked in the side mirror and said I was getting a whole line of cars behind me.

Sweat was pouring from my brow…my arms hurt from the strain of holding onto the steering wheel so tightly in the 10 and 2 o'clock positions. I didn't feel I could take my eyes off the road long enough to check the mirrors but I had too. I glanced up in the rear view and there they were…four or five cars lined up right behind me and we were in a "no passing" zone…I knew 'cause I could see the yellow line on both sides of the middle road marker. I leaned forward…maybe that would give the impression I was going faster.

Two minutes passed…maybe three and I had kept my speed right at thirty-five. Finally Mom let out a sigh and announced if I could not get the speedometer up to 40 she was going to have to take over! She said I was making everybody behind me crazy and I'd better get a move on. I started looking for a place to pull over, but I was afraid if I hit the brakes the guy behind me would run into the back of our truck, so I kept going. Another minute or two went by and Mom was becoming flustered. She scooted over to the middle seat in the cab…took her foot and placed it on top of mine on the gas pedal…then she tromped down hard and the next thing I knew we were doing forty-five. I was screaming at the top of my lungs. She told me to keep it there "or else" and she slid back over to her side of the cab.

I let off a little and she said it's forty five or nothing so I took a big gulp of air and then…and then…I was saved by fate…just as I crested a small hill in front of me there was a farmer on his John Deere. He was pulling a wagon and he had one of those reflective triangles on the back and a sign that said "slow moving vehicle"…whew…I let out a sigh of relief…hit the brakes and slowed way down. I was back into a speed I could handle and I poked along behind the tractor until we got to the outskirts of town. We were just crawling along and all the people behind me had managed to pass us on the straight away. I was feeling pretty relaxed by then so I turned on my signal and pulled over in the church parking lot and killed the engine. I turned over the keys just as we had planned.

Driving the truck wasn't such a big deal…I'd done just fine! I hopped out of the cab and ran around to the other side of the truck. I was thinking I did such a good job mom would probably let me drive home, too! Wow…I'd done so well maybe she'd let me drive the next time we had to go to Chicago to see Sharon. Well…time will tell…guess I'd just have to wait 'n see.

CHAPTER
NINETEEN

SPOOKS
'n THE
NIGHT

The fall after I had gotten my driver's license a bunch of girls decided to go into the big city and see a haunted house being hosted by one of the local radio stations.

Since I had the coolest car...a 69 Mustang...it was decided I should drive.

When we got to the old house that had been artificially "haunted" for the season we all climbed out of the Mustang,...paid our money and waited in line to go in. Of our little group I was the last one in line and when the guy at the door let the bunch in, for some reason, he stopped me and asked me to wait until there was enough room for the next group to go. So I waited...then one of the girls called back to me and he realized we were all together so he told me to go on in and try to catch up with the others.

It was so dark when I first got into the building that I had trouble figuring out where I should be...I could hear the girls ahead of me so I just kept moving forward. I wasn't having a particularly good time 'cause I didn't especially like to be scared. Heck, there were enough things out at the farm that went bump in the night I didn't really think it was necessary to pay money to be scared on purpose.

I was getting a little closer to the familiar sounds of the girls laughing but I still hadn't caught up with them. Suddenly a young man wearing a sweater from one of the local colleges jumped out at me holding a flashlight...I put my hand up over my face to keep the beam of light from blinding me...the man grabbed my right arm pulled it behind my back as he shoved me into a little corner next to a staircase. Right away I knew I was in trouble...I screamed for help…but everyone in the building was screaming for help and no one was paying any attention to me.

I couldn't see exactly where I was but I could see the staircase above me. I was guessing that this guy thought he had me trapped and that he had my strong arm behind my back. But,…I am left-handed…so I doubled up my fist and whopped him right in the face. He started yelling at me and hitting me…I just jumped up and grabbed ahold of the banister over my head…heck I was a working farm girl and I was strong. I held on to the banister tight and started pulling myself up over his head…he grabbed on to my feet and was trying to pull me back down into the black pit.

Just then the baluster of the staircase broke and I fell back down on the floor. The guy kicked me a couple of times and that really scared me…so I stood up and grabbed the board that had come off the staircase…I began to beat this guy about the head and shoulders 'til finally he kicked open a door and we both fell out onto the ground. There was a lot of screaming 'n hollering from both sides and we were rolling around on the grass in a knock down drag out dog fight. I got his sweater up halfway over his head which hampered his ability to fight back, then I beat the daylights out of him with my broken board. In the light from the street lamp I could see he was much bigger than me, and he was older too. I wasn't so scared now that we were out in the open, but I sure was mad. Every time this guy opened his mouth I smacked him again. I started giving him a piece of my mind…I told him he could hurt somebody dragging them around like that! I told him he had pulled my hair! I told him he shouldn't be picking on small defenseless girls…I said he should pick on people his own size. He shook his flashlight at me and I whopped him with my board again.

About that time a policeman came around the corner and demanded to know what was going on. Me 'n the fella both started talking at once. I told the policeman that this man was beating me up! The officer looked at me and saw that I had one small scratch on my neck, then he looked at the man and saw that his arm was bleeding, he had a big knot on his forehead and one eye was beginning to swell shut. He didn't seem too convinced that I was the one getting beat up. At that point the guy I had been wrestling with had the nerve to tell the officer that I had been trying to steal his flashlight!

I said "you big fat liar!" And hit him with my board again! That's when the policeman took my board away from me.

Well I wasn't done with that creepy man yet, so I gave him a good kick and knocked him down on the ground. Then I jumped on his back and pounded him with my fists all the while screaming "TELL – HIM – THE – TRUTH – YOU – BIG – FAT – LIAR!"

The policeman grabbed hold of my sweatshirt and pulled me off. The girls that were with me had finished their tour and wandered back behind the building looking for me. I was huffin' and puffin' and still growling at the kid lying on the ground.

The cop seemed to be unsure of who to believe or what to do next, so he told both of us to go on home. He let go of my shirt and pointed me toward the parking lot, then he hung on to the guy that had pulled me into the corner until I was in the car and driving off.

I drove back to the farm and went into the kitchen and told my momma and daddy about the whole experience. They said they wished they'd been there… that somebody should have done things different, that if they ever saw that guy they would make him hard to catch.

And that was the end of it…well, for a while.

Around Christmas time mom and I were making our weekly laundry run and we had stopped at a store to pick up a few things. As we walked in the door there was a big ladder in the middle of the aisle and a fella hanging up sale signs and Christmas decorations high over our heads. Mom was getting a shopping cart and I was looking at the pretty signs and decorations above me. Then the guy hanging the stuff turned around and started down the ladder…it was THE GUY! It was the guy from the haunted house!

I ran over to my mom, pointed up at the ladder and screamed "there he is momma, there's that man from the haunted house!"

He took one look at me and jumped down off the ladder and started running for the backroom. I was in hot pursuit, and my momma was right behind me. I chased him to the back of the store and right into the stock room. I ran him up an aisle and he fled into the men's bathroom. I followed him in. He ran into a stall…locked the door and said he didn't want anymore trouble with me.

By then me and my momma and the female store manager were all in the men's bathroom. I was pacing back and forth in front of the stall door like a caged lion. I was telling him how he lied to that policeman and how he'd better think twice before he tried to pull a trick like that again! I was hollerin' and the size of the room made my voice echo and boom around us. I told him he had tried to beat me up and he knew it! I told him I never tried to take his stupid flashlight. I told him he owed me an apology and I was going to stand right there until I got it! I told him he could give me one voluntarily or I would beat it out of him!

Mom and the store manager were at the other end of the bathroom talking about the events from the night at the haunted house. I wasn't paying any attention to them, all I was wanted was that guy to fess up to what he'd done to me that night.

For a long while every one was quiet. Pretty soon a thin screechy voice came from the locked stall.

The fellow I had trapped in the bathroom said I must have him mixed up with someone else. I kicked at the stall door. Then he said he had thought I was trying to steal his flashlight. I smacked the door with my fist. With that, he said that he wished he hadn't grabbed me at the haunted house and promised that if I left him alone he would never do anything like that again. He said he hoped I wasn't hurt and he apologized. *Finally*, that's what I'd been waiting for!

I turned around and smiled at my mom.

The store manager told him to come out, and he did. He stood there in the bathroom looking at the floor, and then the manager fired him on the spot.

I walked out of the men's bathroom with my head held high. I left there thinking I had left a lasting impression on him. I decided he got more than he bargained for there at the haunted house.

I realize now that I was pretty naive and more than a little lucky on that fateful Halloween night, and to this day I get downright spooked when I think about what actually could have happened.

CHAPTER
TWENTY

SMOKEY

oris? I've got to tell you some bad news," Mark said over the phone line. I could hear him draw in his breath before finishing the sentence. "Smokey's dead."

"What are you talking about? I rode him yesterday! This is the meanest trick you have ever pulled!" I was sure he could hear the anger in my voice.

"I wouldn't lie to you about this! He's dead...really! He was struck by lightning in the storm...Dad is out there in the woods digging a hole to bury him!"

I asked to speak to mom or dad. Mark said they were out in the woods digging a grave for my horse. He said he'd offered to come up to the house and call me.

I hung-up the phone in disbelief. I got in my car and drove the forty-five minutes it took to get home...crying all the way. Every time I saw Smokey I always had the same greeting. "How you doing, boy? Are you doing okay?" Smokey would nod his head and I believed he was acknowledging my question and telling me he was fine and glad to see me. We'd performed the same routine just the day before and I kept telling myself he was still fine...still okay.

When I pulled up in the barn lot, I immediately jumped out of my car and started running toward the woods. I knew exactly where he'd be...Smokey always liked hanging out by the creek near the hollow oak tree. When I rounded the bend in the creek, I expected to see him standing there, grazing on Kentucky blue grass.

But Smokey wasn't anywhere to be seen. Instead, my folks were there with Mark...the John Deere was running…making its familiar popping sound, and there was a mound of dirt just beneath the old oak. Mark had told the truth.

I stood there shaking my head in disbelief. For the past thirteen years I had spent all my time with that horse. When times were good…Smokey and I celebrated together. When times were bad,…I could stand with his head over my shoulder and cry. He was so much more than a horse to me. Even after I married and moved away, I still came back and rode him almost everyday.

We'd done almost everything together. I used to ride him bareback out to the fields…then lay back with my head on his rump and take naps. Sometimes we'd ride in complete silence…taking in the beauty of the day…we'd run through the fields as fast as the wind 'til both of us were gasping for air. We'd ride out to the woods together and I'd read as he wandered around the creek eating grass and nudging me when it was time to go home. And I always told him all of my deepest, darkest secrets…I told him about the kids who'd teased me…about my failures and successes…about my boyfriends when I got older…about the one I picked to marry and I told him how I suffered when that marriage didn't last. After my baby died, Smokey was the one I turned to for support…together we rode day after day…he was the only one I could tell about how empty I felt and it didn't matter if I sobbed or yelled or screamed out in anger and frustration…he was always there for me and with his soft nose pressed against my shoulder everything seemed better…I knew that, no matter what, he loved me.

We'd been through a lot, Smokey and me. I'd gotten him as a child, and we'd grown up together. He'd been with me through all the pains of being a teenager and stayed with me as I moved into adulthood. Somehow I'd never considered the fact that a day would come when we would not be together.

All I could do was stand there under the old oak tree with a lump stuck in my throat and an ache in my heart staring at his grave. Finally Mom said there was nothing more we could do, so we'd might as well get back up to the house...she and I started walking up the path next to the creek while Mark and Dad crawled up on the John Deere and headed back out through the fields.

As Mom and I got back to the barn lot Dad was just putting away the tractor...I looked over at him...neither of us could think of what to say.

I walked with a heavy heart into the barn...took down Smokey's saddle and plopped it into the trunk of my car. I slammed the trunk closed...crossed my arms over my chest and looked out over the fields where Smokey and I had ridden so many times together. Tears welled up and my heart pounded...finally I couldn't bear to stand there any longer so I got into my car and drove up to the house to say good-bye to my mom.

I walked back down the long sidewalk to my car where Dad was standing in his coveralls all covered in dirt...I looked up into his eyes...the tears were running down my face as I held my breath trying to think of what to say. "Thank you" as all I could manage to croak.

Daddy reached up and pulled Smokey's bridle off his shoulder and handed it to me. The long black leather reins drug on the gravel as I took it from his hand.

"You're gonna be okay, Dorsey-O" Dad said. He slipped his arm around my shoulder and gave me a squeeze. "It's been a tough day...but it'll pass."

I nodded and looked down at the ground. Dad patted my back...then turned and started toward the house. As I took my place behind the wheel of my car a glorious sunbeam shown down on the field where Smokey and I had spent so much time.

I glanced over to the bit and the old leather satchel I'd always carried whenever we rode...as I turned the corner from the lane to the blacktop the satchel fell on the floorboard of the car and my treasures from our ride the day before spilt out. There were two rocks from the creek that I had thought were pretty...a stick I'd used when Smokey was being stubborn, and a four leaf clover that I had found just yesterday, on our last afternoon together.

Twenty-five years have come and gone since that day. I no longer know what happened to the rocks...as for the stick...I threw the stick away on my way home that afternoon because I felt guilty for ever hitting him with it to make him move a little faster. And the four leaf clover...well it still sits on my desk to this day...it's black and faded now...pressed in a pink and green plaid picture frame. Each time I look at it I smile and think of that lazy spring day in the clearing...me crawling around on my hands and knees looking for four leaf clovers…Smokey nuzzling me with his nose and eating the grass.

And every once in awhile I say to him out loud… "Hey boy, how you doing? Don't worry about me, I'm still okay."

Epilogue

The other day I was thinking about Smokey as I drove out to the old farm to visit his grave. My nephew owns the place now, and he's told me lots of times to come on out whenever I feel the need.

No one was home when I got up to the house and from the outside it still has the same look about it. But they are fixing the place up...new windows...floors...walls...the whole works. The place where time stood still is being brought up to date. I know it needs to be done, but there is a sadness about it.

There is something missing when the screen door doesn't slam behind you on your way out of the house or when the windows are all straight and can be opened without raising a sweat or when the sidewalk is aggregate concrete instead of old lopsided bricks.

Without the big truck batteries lined up on chargers on the back porch...without the coveralls hanging side by side next to the back door...without Smokey's bridle waiting by the steps...well, it just isn't the same old place. It isn't home to me anymore.

The old pump handle on the well still looked the same though, and with a little elbow grease I was able to get the water to flow from its red spout. I cupped my hands and took a drink of the cold well-water. The pump groaned and squalled as I pumped the long handle up and down, and I thought of how many times we'd done that same task over the years. I remembered how we would sit the buckets under the spout and then drag them up the hill each day when we first moved to this place. I wondered if I was strong enough to do those chores still today, and I was glad I would probably never have to find out if I could.

I parked my van in the barn lot and started toward the woods. The old tractor path that ran beside the fields is more like a well manicured road. The barn that used to moan and creak in the wind has been rebuilt and is more solid. When I came up on what used to be our orchard, I shook my head, because most of the fruit trees are gone. A clean meadow is all that remains. Without the livestock to keep the weeds down on the little pathways the woods has changed over the years, but I could still find my way.

I took my time wandering along the side of the creek and watched the water bugs dart from one side of the water, between the rocks, zipping over to the other side of the creek. There in the solitude of the woods I let myself daydream about all the times I had there, all the things I'd done over the years.

As I rounded the bend I could see the trunk of the old oak that had fallen across the creek. At the roots of that toppled tree was Smokey's unmarked grave.

I took my seat, and started up my conversation. "How ya doin' boy? I've been doin' okay."

I picked a black-eyed Susan that had grown next to the creek, and pulled on it's petals as I talked. I told Smokey about all the places I'd been this last year, about the kids

I'd met who had stubborn horses like him. I talked about the stories I'd written, and about the ones I am still gonna' get too eventually.

Then I asked him if he remembered how we used to chase the sunbeams. All of my childhood I believed God was in the sunbeams. I can remember how I used to chase them in the fields as I rode Smokey. How we'd move in one until a cloud would block the sun from our faces, sending us in search of the next opportunity. I believed that in that precise moment...just as the sunbeam would fall on us...that we were being blessed by God for our special day. I would always stay in a sunbeam as long as I could to be sure I'd gotten every drop of the blessing...then I'd offer up my little prayer of thanks that God had taken the time to think of me. Somehow no matter what happens in my life, as long as I can find a sunbeam I know everything is going to turn out fine.

I talked a little longer...I told Smokey about dad, and how I wished he'd lived long enough to read my books, and how I thought he would've had a bunch of stories to add to mine. I told a few of dad's favorite tales right there in the middle of the woods to an audience of birds and squirrels, and through the laughter of his stories I felt closer to him.

It wasn't long before I had said all I came to say, cried out all I needed to cry out, and laughed all I could laugh too. The gray clouds were starting to roll in so I figured I'd better head on home. I stood up and told Smoke I missed him and that I'd be back again in the fall. I started to walk away and then I turned and asked Smokey if he missed me too...

that's when
the clouds parted and
a sunbeam kissed my face.

D. D. Dunn lives in Davenport, Iowa,
with her husband Marc
and their youngest daughter.

For more information or to
schedule a speaking event please visit
her website at www.dddunn.com.

If you enjoyed this book and
haven't had a chance to read D.D.'s first book
Binder Twine 'n Bandaids
Homegrown Humor From The Heartland
please visit www.dddunn.com.